What We Are FOR

What
We
Are
FOR

Arthur
Larson

Harper &
Brothers
New York

WHAT WE ARE FOR
Copyright © 1959 by Arthur Larson
Printed in the United States of America

FIRST EDITION
M-H

Library of Congress catalog card number: 59–6004

Contents

What We Are FOR

Chapter

ONE

Why We Must State What We Are For

Stop a man on the street and ask him, "In the world struggle of ideas, what are we against?" The answer will be quick and confident: "Communism."

Now ask him, "And what are we *for?*" The answer will be something like this: "Well, uh, that's a little hard to sum up—after all—it's pretty complicated—we can't just wrap it all up the way the Communists do—" and so on.

This may sound like a harmless little colloquy. But it is the prototype of a problem which, expanded on the national and international scene, may in the years ahead hold the key to felicity or misery for all of us. We must, as a nation and as a people, discover and articulate clearly and affirmatively what we stand for and where we are going.

We can neither make the day-to-day decisions at home on which the optimum development of our own society depends, nor succeed in the contest of ideas overseas, unless we can state what we are for.

Since it has seemed much easier to say what we are against than what we are for, we have often lapsed into the tragic error of justifying our finest activities in negative and defensive terms.

We must have economic aid to newly-developing countries. Why? To counter Soviet economic penetration.

We need a cultural program abroad. Why? To counter the Soviet cultural offensive.

We must have a system of overseas libraries and information. Why? To counter Soviet propaganda—so Congress and the public have been told.

More recently, the same theme appears in connection with domestic issues. We must raise our educational standards. Why? To counter Soviet educational gains.

The net impression left by all this is that the active force for change in the world is Communism, while we, by contrast, represent a rather amorphous, ill-defined force for countering change.

The trouble with this is that most people in the world *want* change. And you can not blame them.

This is particularly true of the people of Asia, Africa, and Latin America, but it is also true of most other people around the globe—including most Americans.

And so, if we get maneuvered into the position of seeming to be anti-change, while our opponents are pro-change, we enter any competition for the minds and hearts of the world's people with a hopeless handicap.

The truth is that what we are for *is* the active, positive force for change in the world. This country's historic and continuing success in practical democracy and widely-shared industrial progress has for years been an explosive force inspiring dozens of other colonies and countries.

Why, then, should there be danger of appearing to yield this role of active force to international Communism?

It is because we have failed to state plainly, positively, and excitingly what we are for.

In the precious years following World War II, when the current contest of ideas was taking form, this country had its spell of McCarthyism. Because, as our man-in-the-street vignette indicates, "against" is so much easier than "for," the energies that during this critical period should have gone into generous, intelligent, positive *actions* to achieve mutual understanding around the world were too often frittered away in negative, frenetic, utterly barren *reactions* to the ideology of Communism.

We have put the McCarthy era behind us, but the dead weight of a decade of negativism is not easily thrown off.

It is not enough merely to shake off this defensive mood. We must catch fire with the white-hot ambitions and inspirations that have rocketed our society to once undreamed-of heights and can raise it and all the world to other heights that are even now almost unimaginable. We must remind ourselves that we are revolutionaries and pioneers, and the sons of revolutionaries and pioneers, and that we have reached only a precarious midpoint in the most radical political-economic experiment in centuries.

As we state what we are for, we must be sure we know precisely what we are trying to accomplish overseas by so doing.

The key lies in one word: "identification."

We are not trying to get India or Viet Nam or the Sudan to imitate us, or to try to duplicate American conditions and methods on Asian or African soil. We know this is impossible. It would be presumptuous of us to attempt to bring it about even if it were possible.

4

And we are not talking about ourselves because of any illusion that everyone on earth is smitten with an unquenchable thirst to know all about us out of sheer intellectual curiosity. Nor are we attempting to create admiration, astonishment, or affection.

Perhaps the simplest way to put it is this: We want to have a feeling, in relation to people of other countries, of "we." Not "we" and "they."

We know that we have differences. But identification means understanding the common principles that we believe in and that bind us together. It means a realization that what we in the United States are for will advance the hopes and plans of these other countries.

If we could once and for all become suffused with this concept of identification, we would instinctively correct some of our commonest blunders. For example, one intrinsically difficult assignment in identification is with the people of the East. Yet what do we do? We proceed to adopt a terminology in which the entire world struggle is summed up as a contest of West against East! And we hand Russia, on a silver platter, the label "East." Now the true fact is that Russia is a white, Western country in the same sense that Germany, England, France and the United States are. Russia's only claim of association with "East" is her imperial conquest of Kazakhs,

5

Turkmenians, Kirghiz, Tadzhiks, Uzbeks and other Asians, who are even now for all practical purposes ruled by non-Asian Russians. This no more makes Russia "East" than the British Empire makes Britain "East."

Understanding Ourselves

Before we can hope to be understood abroad, we must understand ourselves.

We want to identify ourselves with other peoples. Yet too often we ourselves make this almost impossible—not because of real differences, but because of differences inherent in a fictitious picture we have created of ourselves.

There have been quite a few books, pamphlets, and even courses of instruction which set themselves the task of explaining "what we are for."

Some of these statements are eloquent on the great principles of liberty, individuality, religious freedom, and private enterprise. As Chesterton said when comparing the works of George Bernard Shaw with the Venus de Milo, everything that is there is perfect.

But the omissions frequently leave an impression that is so out of date that it is dangerously misleading. You could read some of these statements and never learn that the United States government does in fact regulate, stimulate, and even subsidize American business and agricul-

6

ture in a thousand ways, large and small. You would never know that social insurance exists in the United States—far less that we have one of the world's most highly developed systems. You could be quite unaware of the vital roles played by organized labor, by federal tax, credit, and purchasing policies, and by such agencies as the F.T.C. and the F.P.C., the F.C.C. and the I.C.C., the S.E.C. and the A.E.C., the C.A.A. and the C.A.B., the F.C.A. and the H.H.F.A., the N.L.R.B. and the R.R.B., the V.A. and the S.B.A.

The economics reflected in these statements are much closer to Adam Smith than to Arthur Burns. The agriculture is closer to the Homestead Act than to the soil bank. And as for the role of labor, we are made to seem closer to Walden Pond than to the Wagner Labor Relations Act.

Now, suppose we go to a country like India with this picture of what we are for—a sort of ineffable distillation of purest untrammeled free enterprise, with a laissez-faire government standing benevolently by.

What can India say? She will be driven to say, "We're sorry, but if that really is your system—while it may have worked for you—it cannot possibly fill the bill for us."

India has few capitalists, and very few of the other

ingredients of an American type of self-started, self-propelled private enterprise economic development. She cannot possibly carry forward her plans for industrialization and development without a considerable degree of governmental involvement.

Therefore, if we create the impression that strong government involvement in the economy puts a system beyond the pale, so far as we are concerned, our hopes of identification will be shattered.

Meanwhile, the Communists are saying to these countries, "You need a heavy degree of government participation in economic development; we stand for complete government control of the economy. You're really closer to us."

If we ever let matters get in that state, we would be guilty of one of history's most tragically inexcusable blunders.

The misunderstanding is compounded by the Indian habit of describing their own aspirations as "socialistic," and by verbally rejecting "capitalism"—which to them means mostly pawnbrokers, unscrupulous moneylenders, and the predatory capitalism of which they have learned through Marx.

But when the semantic fog is blown aside, the "socialism" the Indians are talking about turns out to be something quite different from either dictionary socialism or Communist socialism. It is a combination of "social" measures and governmental exertions aimed at "social justice" and "social security."

Of course, in a country like India, there is at this point a considerable need for governmental financing and ownership of heavier industries. But the entire public sector of the Indian economy adds up, as of to-day, to something between 5 and 10 per cent of the whole, including nationalized railroads and communication facilities. It is possible to compile statistics showing that the public sector in the United States may be as great as 18 to 20 per cent of the economy.

Just as the "socialism" India accepts is not really the socialism we reject, so also the "capitalism" India rejects does not resemble at all the "capitalism" mid-century America accepts.

And so, while India utters "socialistic" aspirations and views "capitalism" with alarm, and while we profess "capitalism" and view "socialism" with suspicion, the plain fact is that what the Indians really want is essentially what we ourselves stand for and are continually striving to attain.

One of our major assignments, then, is to cut through out-of-date myths about ourselves and deceptive labels which serve only to create divergence where it does not in fact exist. We need a fresh image of ourselves, and some fresh words to describe it.

In addition, if we make identification our watchword, we will learn another essential lesson. We shall succeed much better in identifying ourselves with others if we candidly admit that we have imperfections and unsolved problems of our own.

There is no warmer bond in human experience than the bond that comes of sharing trouble.

Conversely, there is no colder emotion than the grudging admiration of remote and unattainable good fortune.

So far as the United States is concerned, there is far too much of the latter around the world, and not enough of the former.

In March, 1958, the readers of the British periodical *New Statesman* were startled to encounter an article entitled "I Like America." Hastening to investigate such an uncharacteristic piece in this magazine, they found that the author, Alexander Werth, apparently felt the first real stirrings of affection for Americans when he discovered that they could actually be poor and unhappy. He wrote:

The Americans we meet in Europe all look healthy, wealthy,

and self-assured. I got my first real surprise when I met Frank. "Surely," I said to myself, "no *American* could be so unhappy!" An idiotic reflection, I know, but there it is.

But if we stopped here and merely sought the kinship of imperfection we would miss the whole point of this identification. The important point is to go on from here and show that we are facing up to our unfinished business, and seeking and finding ways of cleaning up our bad spots.

Our hardships and difficulties, then, so far as our image in the eyes of people overseas is concerned, are not a disgrace but a key to mutual understanding.

Who's Got the Ideology?

The most common excuse for our failure to explain what we are for runs like this:

The Communists, it is said, have an advantage in that they peddle a single panacea in a pat, shining package. Its formulas, however unsound in fact, are easily understood, and are guaranteed by them to cure all ills, from poverty and hunger to oppression and war.

By contrast, so our excuse runs, what we stand for is so complex and diversified that we simply cannot wrap it up and present it as an identifiable ideology.

When Americans do manage to formulate an answer

to the question "What are we for?" the replies are apt
to be as varied as the backgrounds of the answerers.

"Capitalism," says the businessman.

"Rule of law," says the lawyer.

"Democratic government," says the political scientist.

"Primacy of the individual," says the philosopher.

"Religious faith," says the preacher.

Some writers, in their zeal to contrast our system with
the planned societies of the dictators, seem to conclude
that our ultimate direction and goal can never be stated,
since they are only a by-product of the decisions of millions of persons within a framework of law.

When all these complications have been acknowledged,
they prove only one thing: not that we cannot effectively
state what we are for, but only that the job is a hard
one.

Although it has become habitual to say that the Russians have an ideology and we do not, a "switch" on this
assumption brings us nearer the truth.

If by "ideology" is meant a set of principles which
have, first, some claim to originality, and, second, some
reasonable relation to practice, then the true fact is that
the ideological advantage is with us.

We in fact have an ideology—which we have not articulated.

12

The Soviets have articulated an ideology—which does not exist in fact.

The Economic Problem as a Proving Ground

To develop this theme, let us begin by using as a proving ground one major segment of the competing systems: the economic.

There is good reason for selecting this segment for primary analysis, for the economic problem appears to be overshadowing all others in the minds of the people about whom we are most concerned.

In the newly-developing countries of Asia and Africa, the passionate determination of their leaders to industrialize, to improve their agriculture and to elevate their standards of living, health, education, and production consumes the greatest part of their thought and energy. The decision whether to become associated with the American or Soviet system of thought and government will probably turn more upon what the aspiring country believes about the relative ability of the systems to solve the economic problem than upon any other factor.

Accustomed as we are to the environment of the industrial, atomic, and outer-space age, we are inclined to overlook the fact that about two-thirds of the world's people are living under conditions not essentially different from those prevailing five thousand years ago. Per capita income in most of the countries of the Middle East, South Asia, and Southeast Asia averages somewhere between a dime and a quarter a day.

But now this five-thousand-year sleep has been broken. Twenty new countries have achieved independence since World War II. An educated class is growing up, and through modern communication and travel large numbers of the people are beginning to learn what they are missing and what their potentialities really are.

Recognizing all this, the Soviets make the following appeal throughout the area: "Look at us. A few decades ago we were an agrarian country like you. Now we are an industrial and scientific giant. True, the United States is a big industrial power too. But their development evolved gradually over a hundred years. You cannot wait that long. Your best hope is to throw in your lot with us and adopt our methods."

If they succeed in this line of argument, the rightness or wrongness of other parts of the ideological position may fade out of sight.

This is not to say that the newly-developing countries are determined to have material progress at any cost, and that they are willing to sacrifice, as the Communist countries have done, freedom, justice, religion, and personal rights. On the contrary, the countries of the free world are determined to have their economic development and their freedom too.

But right now they do not need any homilies from us on the beauties of freedom and the horrors of servitude. They agree completely that freedom is precious. Most of them have just emerged from a long struggle for national freedom. A surprising number of their leaders have moved fairly directly from colonial jails to chancelleries. They are not apt to part with freedom lightly.

The desirability of freedom, then, is not what is being currently put to the test. The test is: Can the desired rapid economic development be achieved under a system which, like ours, simultaneously gives expression to freedom, justice, religion, and human personality?

The answer given in this book is that we have indeed evolved a system whose principles, with allowance for differing conditions and stages of development, are generally valid not only for us but for other countries.

For convenience, this system may be given the name "Enterprise Democracy."

Chapter

TWO

Enterprise Democracy

In the all-important field of the relation of government to people and to business in a modern industrial society, America has a new and epoch-making idea to contribute: Enterprise Democracy. It is not socialism, creeping or any other kind. It is not the classical capitalism of Marx and Adam Smith. It is not a mixture of the two. Nor is it "going down the road" to one or the other. It is a thing in itself.

The key to enterprise democracy is the "Lincoln formula."

Lincoln said that the function of government is to do

for people what needs to be done, but what they cannot do at all for themselves, or do so well.

Implicit in this principle are three ideas of significance in the current question of the relation of government to people and to the economy.

The first idea is that in a modern industrial society there should be more than one entity acting upon the needs of people.

The second idea is that the major entities in a modern industrial society are not basically in conflict with each other, but rather support each other.

The third idea is that there is an inherent preference in favor of the private as against the governmental way of doing things.

Let us look at these three ideas in more detail.

The Pluralism of Modern Industrial Society

There are three major independent components in modern economic life: business, government, and labor. Any ideology or political structure which ignores this fact is dangerously out of date. This includes Communism, which is still based upon the conditions of 1859 rather than those of 1959.

In classical capitalism, it was taken for granted that only one force counted in the economy: private business.

So far as government was concerned, it had no function except to keep hands off. So far as labor was concerned, it was a commodity to be purchased just as materials were purchased.

The Communists turned all this upside down in their theories—but retained the error of recognizing only one force. That force was the government. Business and labor lost their identity within the totalitarian state.

Then a third element made its appearance: strong, organized labor, as a force separate from both of the others —a development which does not figure in the calculations of either the 1859 capitalists or the 1859 Communists.

The Mutual-Interest Concept of Enterprise Democracy

The old view was one based on inherent antipathy between business and the other two elements.

The class struggle between capital and labor was accepted as a fact of life by both sides. At one extreme, fanatical Communists were willing to destroy the employer to gain their ends, while at the other the nineteenth-century capitalist was presumed to have no interest in labor except to wring as much exertion from it as possible for the lowest possible wage.

Similarly, both sides agreed that the relation between government and business was one of enmity. The employers dealt with government on the assumption that any government involvement in business affairs was an evil, poisonous thing. The Communists expressed the essential antagonism in another way, contending that the government should destroy and take over private business.

Now, a novel and distinctive contribution of American thought is this: The three elements in modern industry —private enterprise, organized labor, and government— far from being fundamentally antagonistic, are fundamentally mutually helpful, and indeed essential to the highest realization of the interests of each other. Their function is not to thwart or displace each other. Their function is to support each other. Rightly conceived, with proper leadership, and with an intelligent sense of self-interest in each case, these three forces have ultimately a common interest. By recognizing their proper roles and the roles of the other forces, and by playing their parts in advancing the mutual interest, these three elements can raise the standards of production and prosperity far beyond the level that could be attained by any one of them, no matter how unlimited the power and freedom given to that one might be.

Let us look at several examples.

Mutual Interest in Government Regulation of Business

Private enterprise under mid-twentieth-century conditions could not function, much less flourish, without a high degree of government regulation.

Take one of our newer industries: radio and television. How could it exist without apportionment of wave lengths and channels by the government? Try to imagine a television industry growing up on an every-man-for-himself basis, with the airwaves made hideous by the congested signals of competitors trying to drown each other out.

Or consider the packaged food and cosmetics business. In simpler times, the purchaser examined the food he bought, and could consider the grocer or butcher directly responsible for the food he sold. Nowadays, it never occurs to the buyer to question the wholesomeness of the contents of a jar of pickles, and it seldom occurs to the grocer to assume any responsibility for it. Somewhere in the remote distance, separated by layers of processors and middlemen, is the original producer of the pickles. Hovering protectively over the scene is the unseen form of the government inspector. And so, with confidence born of government inspection, Food and Drug Acts, and a whole network of governmental involvement, the ultimate consumer freely buys packaged goods—and a gigantic and wealth-producing industry is made possible.

It comes to this: If you want to have an economy which sells its pickles in sealed jars, you must also accept an economy in which government standards and regulations are normal. Under a strict laissez-faire concept of government, business could never rise above the pickle-barrel stage. Only with the aid of government can it achieve the age of mass distribution and supermarkets.

It need hardly be added, of course, that if government activity goes one inch beyond what is clearly necessary to do this kind of job in the interest of the public, then its effect does indeed become harmful and stifling, as it often was in medieval times, and still is in some countries.

Similarly, air travel can grow up and expand—because the government regulates air traffic, investigates accidents, and enforces safety standards.

Small investors buy stocks and bonds, because securities legislation polices the truth of prospectuses and the honesty of stock-market trading.

The oil business avoids utter chaos because of governmental rules on production quotas—made necessary by the very nature of the business, in which great underground pools of oil extending over thousands of acres could physically be pumped by any person who happened to own a large enough part of the surface to put down the four legs of an oil rig.

The oil industry might well be examined a little more closely, as an example of an industry which most people would probably consider a typical private, rugged-individualist business.

The fact is that this business is laced through and through with government regulation, most of it as the result of the industry's own request, following the chaotic conditions of the early thirties. Supply and demand are brought into rough balance by a complex process which begins when the Department of the Interior estimates probable demand for oil and oil products for a particular month. Then an interstate agreement between the oil-producing states goes into play—an agreement approved by Congress. The enforcement rests on a law forbidding the transportation in interstate commerce of oil produced in amounts above the "allowables" for the state. Here, then, is a cooperative system administered by the industry, the state governments, and the federal government—not to hurt the industry, but to help it operate as a private enterprise business.

As long, then, as the government confines itself to

22

those activities which are necessary in the interest of business itself and in the public interest, it is clear that government and business are mutually beneficial forces.

Mutual Interest in Social Insurance

There was a time when businessmen seemed to assume that some dimly-understood law of nature required them always to be against unemployment insurance, workmen's compensation, disability insurance, and social security.

Let us look at the real function performed by social insurance in today's private enterprise system.

America's high-level economic activity—and this is a fair description in spite of particular ups and downs—is first of all a consumer-based prosperity. This is clear from the kinds of goods and services produced and the proportion that go into meeting the needs and wants of consumers.

This consumer-based prosperity, in turn, is possible to a considerable degree because of installment buying. The large expenditures, such as for houses, cars, and major appliances, are typically made possible by time-payment plans.

Installment buying, in its turn, is possible only in a system which provides reasonable continuity of income and, even more important, a confident expectation of continuity of income.

Continuity of income, and the expectation of continuity of income, finally, are possible only, for most people, because they have social insurance. If a wage earner had no unemployment insurance, no workmen's compensation, and no disability insurance, he would not dare to commit himself to monthly payments stretching out over a period of years. Any substantial spell of unemployment or illness would mean forfeiting both the goods and perhaps most of the payments. But with a set of social insurances providing at least a good fraction of his usual income during these periods of wage-interruption, the wage earner can with confidence buy the things he wants and needs, enjoy them, pay for them, and at the same time keep the American economy humming in high gear.

It is time we faced up squarely to the fact that, while our *production* system is based almost entirely on labor obtained on a per-hour basis, our *distribution* system is based on the tacit assumption that most Americans live on the equivalent of an annual salary.

The per-hour method of engaging the services of labor has tremendous advantages for production in the flexibility it affords.

The assumption of a continuous income also has tremendous advantages for distribution, in that it permits people to buy large items that they would have to do without for years if required to pay for them with cash.

The link that makes it possible to have both advantages is social insurance.

There are many other ways in which income insurance supports business, most of them well known, and becoming better known each time we have another recession.

In every recent recession, one of the most astonishing apparent paradoxes has been the smallness of the decrease in personal income and consumer spending compared with the greatness of the increase in unemployment. In 1958, for example, personal income at its lowest point was down only 1½ per cent from the start of the recession, and on an annual basis was down only something like one half of one per cent. A large part of the reason is income insurance, principally unemployment insurance. The cushioning effect of pouring billions of dollars into the purchasing stream automatically, at exactly the right time and in the right places, through unemployment insurance, is now accepted by almost everyone as one of the principal reasons why modern recessions do not spiral downward into severe depressions.

One other advantage to business may be mentioned:

the facilitating of the maximum use of our manpower and skills. Unemployed skilled workers are not required to seize upon the first job that comes along, however far removed from their training and talent. They can without penalty wait a reasonable time for something suited to their prior experience. This means that valuable skills are not dissipated through desperation.

Suppose, for example, that during a major automobile layoff in Detroit the trained workers had no source of income. What would happen? They would scatter to the four winds in search of any kind of job that would keep them from starving. Machinists would dig ditches in New Mexico. Patternmakers would wash dishes in Alabama. Then, when the manufacturer was once more able to resume production, his trained work force would be gone, and he would have the staggering task of reassembling another from the ground up. As it is now, he can get his trained workers back, in exactly the skills and numbers needed, on a few hours' notice.

Although the benefit to business is the most conspicuous in the case of unemployment insurance, the other social insurances perform a similar function.

The basic function of preserving continuity of income, and confidence in continuity of income, is performed just as much by workmen's compensation, sickness and disability insurance for non-occupational disability, old age pensions, and survivors' insurance. In all these cases, the principle is the same. Normal income is interrupted or stopped by some event—unemployment, illness, work accident, old age, or death. The insurance guarantees that a substantial fraction of average wage will continue during the income interruption.

Even as an anti-recession measure, all these systems play a part. For one thing, they provide a continuing flow of income, at the rate of 23 billion dollars a year in 1958, that is not affected by the ups and downs of the business cycle. Moreover, this income is in the hands of people who would often be the first to be hit by any kind of business adversity—the older, the less fit, and other marginal workers. In addition, it should be remembered that if these people, now on social security or workmen's compensation, did not have a source of income in social insurance, they would in most cases probably be dependent on some wage earner, just as in pre-social-insurance days the old folks and the disabled simply moved in with children or relations. If this were the case, for every one active wage earner who lost his job during a recession, you would create not just one income-less person, but perhaps several. The effect of unemployment would be multiplied substantially beyond its present effect. But, in a well-rounded social insurance system, the millions of disabled, retired, and dependent persons, instead of becoming a multiplier of the effects of unemployment, become just the opposite—a steadying force of continuity of income and spending.

The example of social insurance has been developed at length because it provides an excellent test case of our central principle: the principle that the ultimate interests of government, labor, and business reinforce rather than combat each other. If the principle is clearly accepted in this area, where antagonism has so often in the past been taken for granted, we are well on our way toward acceptance of the principle as a general truth.

The Mutual Interests of Business and Labor

On the surface, of course, is the perennial struggle between management and unions over the size of wages and other benefits. But to equate this with a class struggle, in which the two contenders have flatly opposite ultimate interests—indeed, in which the one conceives its goal to be the destruction of the other—is wrong.

The Marxian view appeared to assume a fixed amount of wealth to be enjoyed. The problem then was simply that of taking it away from the capitalists and giving it to the workers, through expropriation and nationalization. Marx, like most writers on economics prior to John Stuart Mill, was preoccupied with the problem of distribution and paid far too little attention to the matter of production.

The modern American view is that the interests of management and labor are basically the same: more production for all to share.

The best proof of the contention that organized labor is good for business is the over-all story of American business progress in the places where organized labor has been strong.

If we concede that our consumer-based prosperity is dependent on widespread possession of purchasing power that is both high and dependable, and if we agree further that this high and dependable purchasing power is to a large degree the result of the bargaining power exerted over the years by organized labor, it becomes apparent that there is a direct causal relation between strong labor and good business. Now, very few people will dispute the first assumption, but some will dispute the second. Some employers will contend that wages and benefits would have been raised to these levels anyway, and isolated examples like Henry Ford's five-dollar day can be found to support the contention. But the very sensation accompanying this voluntary wage increase is the best evidence that it was exceptional rather than typical.

In addition, business is helped by organized labor in many lesser ways—in the stabilizing of its manpower problems, in the elimination of a multitude of small and irresponsible outbreaks, in the establishment of orderly machinery for the handling of everyday grievances, and so on.

The Obsolescence of the Marx-Hegel Idea of Conflict

It will be noticed that the philosophical beginning point of this view of the mutual interests of government, business, and labor is at the opposite pole from the Marx-Hegel dialectic which has colored most political thought since the time of Marx.

This view pictured history as a series of head-on collisions between bitterly opposed forces, resulting in a smashup which thereupon somehow led to the emergence of a new Something on a higher plane.

This is not the place to analyze the validity of this concept in its application to all past history. But two things are clear:

The first is that, in its Marxian application to the class struggle, it has not worked out according to the blueprint. The forces of capital and labor, instead of plunging relentlessly into the violent conflict predicted by Marx, found ways of bringing their interests closer together. Labor became stronger and was able to obtain better wages, working conditions, and security. Employers came to feel a greater sense of responsibility for the human needs and rights of their employees. The community developed higher expectations about working environment and living standards. The government provided social and labor legislation aiding this process of amelioration of the conditions under which work was performed.

The events of the past hundred years, then, disprove Marx's theory that the higher order is born of a violent clash between antipathetic forces that have run their course. These events equally clearly prove that, under modern conditions, a higher order is reached when apparently opposing forces learn to discover their common interests and to support each other in the common upward movement.

The dialectical interpretation of events is not only discredited by the experience of the past century; it is discredited in advance as a formula for the coming century.

The reason is this: With the advent of the hydrogen bomb and delivery systems that can carry it in quantity almost anywhere on earth, it has become clear enough that any first-magnitude clash of the Hegel-Marx variety could not possibly give rise to a *tertium quid* superior to the older forces which collided. The idea that some sort of glorious radioactive phoenix might rise from the ashes of total nuclear war is too ridiculous for comment. Indeed, due to their superior capacity for withstanding the effects of radiation, the insects would probably inherit such an earth. And, since they alone among God's creatures seem to have the perfect temperament for collectivism, perhaps in a sense the doctrines of Marx would thus ultimately triumph.

In other words, whether or not the dialectical theory had any plausibility in the past, when conflict even at its worst was by modern standards very limited, this theory cannot be tolerated in the period that lies ahead.

If this simple notion could ever be made to permeate the minds of Communist leaders and theorists, we might begin to make some progress toward reducing world tensions. But official dogma changes slowly. Lenin's words are still sacred, although Lenin obviously did not foresee an era of weapons that could destroy all life on the globe.

Lenin, in the best Marxian tradition, wrote:

. . . the existence of the Soviet Republic side by side with the imperialist states for a long time is unthinkable. In the end either one or the other will conquer. And until that end comes, a series of the most terrible collisions between the Soviet Republic and the bourgeois states is inevitable.

He adds:

If . . . we master all means of warfare, we shall certainly be victorious.

These well-known quotations, and many others like them, reflect the inherent expansionist doctrine of international Communism.

But is anyone in the Kremlin asking himself this blunt question: If we are really talking, not about limited clashes but about the "most terrible collisions" between major powers, and when collisions of these dimensions must almost necessarily turn into virtual annihilation of life on earth, how can the gleaming Communist utopia arise out of this kind of process? Is it not time to reexamine the deepest philosophical underpinnings of Marxism-Leninism, beginning with this assumption of a violent showdown clash, and see whether the entire ideological foundation of Communist expansionism is not rendered preposterous by the hydrogen bomb?

The Roots of the American Mutual-Interest Idea

The only theory, then, which provides explanation for the past century and survival for the next century is the theory, not of implacable class struggle but of the necessity of finding ways to make struggling forces support rather than destroy each other.

It is this kind of theory that has evolved on the soil of America.

The class struggle was never an indigenous American phenomenon.

Certainly we had some of the symptoms of the class struggle. We had some appallingly bad labor conditions. We had some killings and beatings and property destruction in connection with strikes. We had slogans and shoutings from both sides which were in the accepted jargon of Marxism.

But, in the perspective of history, this was a temporary and passing phase and never permeated deeply into American life.

The native American labor movement was something quite different. The early unions, from their first stirrings in the 1820s, would have been horrified if anyone had suggested that their mission was to engage in an all-out fight with employers. The idea of classes simply could not exist in a new world where every man could expect to move freely from one economic stratum to another, and where, except in a few older centers, life did not hold still long enough anywhere to permit social classes to congeal.

It was not until rather late in the century, when there arrived from Europe an unusually large and difficult-to-assimilate flood of laborers, and a considerable flood of Marxian ideas, that we began to experience a period of labor strife resembling that of England and the Continent.

But, not having its roots in American life, this kind of struggle never became ingrained or accepted as an inherent part of our society. By the 1940s, the basic American concept of mutuality of interest was reasserting itself strongly. One of its most eloquent spokesmen is David J. McDonald, president of the United Steelworkers of America. He has flatly rejected the old Marxian attitude which he paraphrases as:

Let's get all we can and the devil take the hindmost. Forget the equities of the owners. Forget the equity of management. Grab what we can, and if necessary, put them out of business.

He goes on to say that every nation which has adopted this predatory philosophy has "swallowed up the trade unions and made men slaves." He adds:

The great corporations of our country are no longer owned by small family groups. Thousands of stockholders own the big corporations, particularly in the steel industry . . .

35

Those stockholders, through the operation of some sort of voting system, employ a group of managers. Those managers are simply employees of the corporations.

Then there is another group of employees known as the working force. Both these groups have this mutual trusteeship and in its operation they are obliged to give full consideration to everyone involved.

Certainly the managers must give full consideration to the just claims of the workers and just as certainly, the working force must see to it that the steel properties are operated successfully because if they are not there will be no jobs.

Both, of course, have an obligation to the owners of stock because if there is no new investment money flowing into the particular company, decadence will set in all over the nation. This we will not stand for.

The author of these words is head of a union many of whose members and officers still personally remember some of the bitterest episodes of the earlier phase, such as the Homestead Strike.

We still have occasional violence. But the authentic voice of American labor is not yesterday's shout of hatred in the heat of a violent struggle. It is today's statesmanlike acceptance of the obligation of the working force toward management and ownership, balancing the corresponding obligation of those entities toward labor.

Probably this tradition of mutual help owes something to pioneer life and the necessities of the typical American community. Nothing is more characteristic of American life than the impulse of the neighbors or the community to come to the aid of a stricken member. If a barn burned, the surrounding farmers rallied and put on a barn-raising bee, giving their labor freely—and in most farm areas they still do this. In town, if a neighbor is disabled by polio or loses all his goods in a fire, someone is almost certain to start up a drive to raise money to help take care of the family.

American life is traditionally intensely competitive. Yet side by side with this competitiveness there is a strong strain of cooperativeness, stemming from an instinctive awareness that the cooperation will raise the fortunes of both competitors to a higher level. For example, in American towns we constantly see all kinds of improvements and events sponsored by the business community as a whole. Each businessman who contributes hard cash to sponsoring a community orchestra or festival or park or college knows that in so doing he is helping all his competitors as well as himself. But he knows that if he helps his competitors and himself the whole community, carrying with it his personal interests, will rise to a higher level.

One could go on multiplying homely illustrations of American traits, customs, and attitudes that confirm this over-all tradition of mutual helpfulness as a way to get ahead. It was America that carried to full flower the idea that, in commercial transactions, instead of trying to skin the customer in any way he could, the seller should rather lavish upon the customer courtesy, service, and attentions of all kinds. It is America that has built its commerce on the slogan that the customer is always right. You do not cheat and trick the customer in order to have the satisfaction of getting the best of him; rather, you wipe his windshield, sweep his floormat, fill his battery, radiator, tires, and windshield-washer free of charge, and provide him a rest room with germ-destroying ultraviolet radiation, in order to have him come back.

The mutual-interest philosophy, then, is not an intellectual abstraction. It is a habit of thought and action that has sprung naturally from American soil, and has been confirmed and accepted as the result of practical experience.

The Presumption in Favor of the Non-Governmental

The recognition by Enterprise Democracy of a positive duty of the government to act upon the needs of people, and of the mutual benefit that flows from such action, is what distinguishes it most sharply from laissez-faire capitalism.

But now we must face in the other direction and stress the feature that distinguishes enterprise democracy equally sharply from Communism and other philosophies of state ownership of all business. That feature is the strong and all-pervading principle that it is better, if possible, to get things done non-governmentally than governmentally.

This is such an ingrained habit of thought with Americans that most of them would probably not think of questioning it. Without asking why, most Americans will immediately protest when the federal government proposes to embark on some new category of activity, such as controls on consumer credit, or some extension of activity, such as added public production of electricity. And there is no surer way to evoke American approval than to announce (as someone does almost every month) that you are going to see to it that the federal employment rolls are slashed by ten per cent.

It is almost incomprehensible to most Americans that there might be people who actually believe that more government is good in itself. Yet there are many people in the world who do believe that the exercise of governmental power is by its nature better than the exercise of private powers. They believe it is somehow purer. They think it is less tainted with crass self-interest and greed. They assume it will be exercised more justly, more in the interests of all the people, more wisely, and even more tastefully.

Leaving aside for the moment one distinction between public and private action—the decisive distinction—we could carry on an interminable and inconclusive debate on whether governmental action is intrinsically better than private.

Are bureaucrats always inefficient, lazy, wasteful, dull, and leaden-eyed, falling over each others' feet as they endlessly move paper from the incoming to the outgoing basket? Are employees of private concerns, such as railroads or dry-cleaning establishments or television repair concerns, invariably alert, brisk, skillful, infallible, prompt, and free from human error? Of course not. Any one of us could tell stories of ability, courage, and sustained hard work on the part of government employees that could not be surpassed by anything out of private life. And we could tell stories all night about inefficiency and stupidity in private firms equaling anything the government is capable of producing.

Does the government have better taste? Well, one could contrast the B.B.C. Third Program with American

soap operas, bracketed and punctuated by endless Niag-
aras of faucet water running over gleaming dishes held in
petal-soft hands. On the other hand, one could display
an impressive roster of American programs—dramatic,
musical, operatic, humorous, public affairs, educational
—and contrast this rich, never-ending variety with the
slim pickings and copious silences offered by public or
semipublic television abroad.

An argument, then, between a devout statist and an
American with his typical aversion to government action
is apt to convince neither if it follows these lines.

Now let us go right to the heart of the matter. Is the
American tradition of instinctive aversion to government
a reasonable one? Or is it an out-of-date individualistic
prejudice? What is there about governmental power
that should provoke such violent feelings of suspicion
and resistance? Why do we not react with equal violence
to the accretion of power to, for example, a great business corporation or a professional association? The National Education Association has far more power over
educational policy than the government will ever have—
yet we see no mass protest on this front. Other entities
—churches, unions, trade associations, business organizations, universities—exercise important powers over the
lives of people. But they never experience the nation-wide

presumption that any increase in their power should automatically be questioned.

The reason for this presumption in the case of government is plain, cogent, and valid.

Government is different from all other entities in one crucial respect: Its power over our freedoms, our fortunes, and our lives can be ultimate and absolute.

Every other power in our society is secondary. The power of government is final. That is why we instinctively resist its increase.

The corporation, the union, the university, the association, even the church—these can take actions that penalize you or restrict you. But there is always some kind of appeal to the courts or to the legislature.

The unique quality of government is that, given the requisite laws, it can imprison you, take your money in taxes, draft you into the Army, and burn you in the electric chair—all legally. No one else can.

The labor union can exact dues from you. But you can always resign from the union. The government exacts taxes from you and you cannot escape by resignation.

The professional society can throw you out. But the government can lock you in—for life.

The university can fail you or expel you. But the government can hang you.

What this means is that, since the government can take your freedom, your property and your life, any new area of control or activity handed over to the government is immediately backed up by this absolute power.

The economic power inherent in a great corporation is formidable. But it must maintain itself by economic means. It cannot—as government can in the final analysis—bolster itself with an army, a taxing power, and a lawmaking power.

Consider what happens, then, when to immense economic power you add the ultimate unqualified power over the liberties, goods, and lives of persons.

If the government goes into business, either in a limited way through selective nationalization of industries, or completely through take-over of all production and distribution, the economic power lodged in the government exerts not only its own intrinsic force—that is, the force of bargaining, business competition, buying power, and the like. It exerts this backed up by the final power to determine controversies of every kind. It exerts this backed up by the legislative power to make all the rules. It exerts this backed by the final power to help itself to as much money as it wants in the form of taxes. It exerts this backed by the final physical authority of the police, the jail, the army, and the gallows.

In the everyday lives of modern men, there are two great forces that bear upon their freedom: the economic and the political.

When these forces are dispersed and balanced in a pluralistic society, you have freedom.

When these forces are combined and concentrated, you have tyranny.

Dispersed and separated, they can check and offset each other.

An eighteenth-century continental monarch might indeed wield great power. But if he had to go to a Rothschild to get loans to finance his plans, his power was far from absolute.

A King Henry might appear to have vast power in England. But if he constantly had to reckon with the burghers and merchants and traders, his power was something short of absolute.

Conversely, an American Telephone and Telegraph Company might seem to have fantastic economic power. It was once said to control wealth of greater value than the property contained within the boundaries of twenty-one states. Yet it must bow as meekly as any hamburger stand operator to any law, regulation, imposition, license, fine, or tax that the tiniest town might choose to place upon it. For the political power has behind it the un-

44

limited and unappealable power of law, force, army, and police.

Now, when the same hands grasp both complete political-military power and complete economic power, as in a thoroughly socialized or communized state, then despotism is absolute.

It is this feature of modern Soviet Communism, this combination of total economic and political power, that makes it a blood-relation of the absolute despotisms of antiquity, rather than of the milder autocracies of less ancient times.

This principle might almost be expressed as an equation:

$$T = E + P.$$

Tyranny equals Economic plus Political Power.

Since the government, through legislative, executive, military and judicial functions, has or can have unlimited powers from which there is no escape, and since the greater includes the less, it follows that it can assume as many and as varied powers short of the absolute as it happens to find convenient.

In so doing, it assumes a posture which bears no relation to the posture of private business or to the laws of economics.

When it goes into business, the government can easily

ensure that it will not fail financially. The government's sources of revenue are not bounded by any business considerations affecting a private enterprise. If the government venture is losing, the gap can be made up out of taxes. Moreover, if the customers do not like the product or service, they can be ignored. If property is needed, there is always the right of eminent domain. If labor is needed, there is always the possibility of slave labor camps and other forms of labor compulsion. If payment on borrowings seems awkward when due, the government can always cancel the obligation.

Then, of course, if anyone complains too much about these things, the government can always lock him up or exile him or shoot him. These things not only can be done. All of them *have* been done in Communist states, behind some kind of façade of legality.

It is an instinctive sense, then, of this unbridgeable difference between government and all other organizations that prompts most of us to rebel automatically against any aggrandizement of governmental activity.

Chapter

THREE

A New Political Yardstick

Enterprise Democracy is new and, as stated earlier, cannot be accurately described as merely a sort of middle position somewhere between statism and laissez-faire capitalism.

If this newness of the American political-economic idea is to be understood, at home or abroad, the indispensable first step is to get away once and for all from the stereotyped notion that all political-economic ideas can be placed on a calibrated scale running from left-wing to right-wing.

This calibration has become so much a part of modern political thought that it will be no easy matter to

47

dislodge it. But dislodged it must be. As long as it persists, the American political scene will remain incomprehensible, not only to people from other countries, but also to ourselves.

Basically the reason is this: The left-right spectrum presupposes the built-in conflicts between private business, on the one hand, and labor or government, on the other. Now if, as we have seen, these forces are not inherently antagonistic, but rather support each other, it is clear at once that a calibration based on the assumption of such a nonexistent fundamental conflict is itself fundamentally irrelevant.

The use of loaded terms such as liberal and conservative is being deliberately avoided here, since by now the problem of definition of these words is beyond all prospect of agreed solution. To equate conservative with right-wing, and liberal with left-wing, as is so often done, serves only to compound the confusion.

Classical liberalism was characterized by an extreme laissez-faire attitude toward governmental involvement in business. By modern left-right tests, it was a right-wing movement.

The foundations of American political thought were laid in rebellion against conservative forces in England, and were replete with concepts which were nothing if not

radical. Therefore, if American conservatism should con-
serve the foundations of American political thought, it
would have to cherish these same radical notions and
oppose the "conservative" forces the founding fathers
revolted against.

So conservative becomes liberal and liberal becomes
conservative, and no one becomes much wiser about the
realities of current political alignment.

The left-right lineup in an industrial society is less
elusive. Essentially it starts from the assumption of a
class struggle between business and labor, and a parallel
struggle between free enterprise and "interfering" government, and then assigns places in the spectrum according to what side is taken in those struggles, and with
what degree of violence, impatience, or arbitrariness.

But if you deny the existence of these struggles, the
unit of measurement itself is seen to be unusable—just
as if you tried to measure the brightness of a lamp with
a tape measure.

And yet, Americans for decades have gone along al-
lowing all political analysis and appraisal to be cast in
left-right terms. Foreign observers come to our shores,
take one look at our apparently crazy mixed-up political
party alignments, and retreat in utter despair of ever
making sense of them. We ourselves, instead of evolving

and articulating a clean-cut indigenous political philosophy that springs from and accounts for our own alignments and differences, obligingly try to cram our structure into the left-right mold, only to discover that you might as well try to force a trombone into a bowling-ball case. Similarly, we waste billions of words and run serious risks of making foolish mistakes by attempting to measure movement and direction with this same invalid left-right test. Over and over again we hear that a particular move is "a sharp swing to the right", or "veering a little to left of center".

Many American intellectuals of the thirties and forties accepted this framework for discussion, so that their only topic for debate was, "Are we headed for Communism in America or Fascism, and how soon will it come?"

As late as 1947, this unsupported but ingrained mental cliché was passing as avant-garde sophistication in such works as Harold Laski's *The American Democracy*. Laski announced that

. . . the history of the United States would, despite everything, follow the general pattern of capitalist democracy in Europe.

The words "despite everything" are a rather poignant little acknowledgment of the fact that, to anyone who cared to look, there was visible a mountain of evidence that the United States was following a pattern of its own, with its own terms, its own timing, its own conflicts, its own interest groupings, and its own temperament.

Instead of having one party on the Right, and another on the Left, or one Conservative party and one Liberal party, our scene displayed, and still displays, two parties each of which accommodates people and views that seem to run the entire range of the "left-right" spectrum. We see a kaleidoscope of apparently inexplicable mixtures of political coloration across the landscape. North Dakota tends to be radical, South Dakota conservative—although nothing divides them but a surveyor's line on the map. Traditional free-trade areas in the south begin to turn protectionist and isolationist. Some Republican farm strongholds go Democratic. Some Democratic urban centers go Republican. Politics makes strange bedfellows on Capitol Hill almost every week. And the lapse of a few months can reshuffle the pattern almost beyond recognition. No sooner have history's most sustained and bitter cries demanding greatly decreased federal spending faded on the autumn air than the winter air is filled with equally sustained and bitter cries by many of the same people demanding greatly increased federal spending.

Where is the "left-wing, right-wing" in all this?

There is a strong temptation to throw up one's hands and conclude that this entire kaleidoscope is utterly incapable of reduction to anything resembling a pattern of principle.

But if we are to reject the left-right calibration—which at least serves some purpose, even if a misleading one—we ought to put something else in its place.

An attempt to do that is going to be made here. But it must be stressed that the most one can aspire to is some pervading principle which can help to explain and grade political-economic ideas in a rough way, realizing that a lot of unclassifiable and inconsistent exceptions will be left unaccounted for by any such attempt.

The calibration here proposed is one which runs, not from right to left, but from a very narrow to a very broad view, in terms of space, interest, and time.

On this scale, you will find most "extremists" of both the conventional Right and Left clustered together at the end marked "narrow."

And you will find many of those who were classed as "middle-of-the-roaders" on the old scale now clustered, on the new scale, not in the middle, but at the extreme end marked "broad."

Rather than elaborate this idea in the abstract, let us try it out on some specific examples.

Reciprocal Trade as a Broad-Narrow Problem

One of the oldest political controversies in this or any other country is that of tariffs and other restrictions on trade with foreign countries. It is also a good example of the exasperating task that confronts anyone who attempts to find a clean left-right or conservative-liberal explanation for the history of an issue. At one time or another, and often at the same time, you could both find free-trade and protectionist sentiment in substantial strength among liberals, among businessmen, among trade unions, among Northerners, among Southerners, among Republicans and among Democrats.

The lineup during the 1958 Congressional debates on extension of the Reciprocal Trade Agreements Act was about as mixed up politically as anyone could imagine. While the President and the titular head of the Democratic Party, Mr. Stevenson, were addressing a conference called to support reciprocal trade, the chairman of the House Republican Campaign Committee was addressing a rival meeting called to fight the bill, and the transition of the traditional free-trade policies of some Southern Democrats toward protectionism was posing a new threat to passage.

What is the principle that sorts all this out? It is the fact that the proponents of increased foreign trade are taking, first, a broad, nationwide view in terms of geography, and second, a long-range view in terms of time. The opponents of increased foreign trade, by contrast, are taking, first, a local view of the adverse effects of freer trade on some mill or mine or industry in their district, and, second, a short-range view in terms of time, as to the best interests even of the people of their own limited district.

The conservative businessman, who perhaps at one time was assumed to be automatically a high-tariff man, now knows that an economy as a whole cannot export without importing, and that an economy cannot go on for many years exporting several times as much as it imports. Therefore he begins to favor reciprocal trade as a national over-all policy. He knows that our economy has expanded and prospered mightily during the years that tariffs have been gradually reduced under the Reciprocal Trade Agreements system. And so we see some of the most powerful business organs and organizations, such as *Business Week,* the *Wall Street Journal,* and the United States Chamber of Commerce, taking their stand squarely in favor of the Reciprocal Trade Agreements Act.

At the same time, we see trade union representatives representing small local unions, whose workers are employed in local plants that might be hit by import competition, right out in the forefront of the fight for protectionism, although national labor leadership is pursuing the opposite policy. The reason is again obvious. It is not that the local union is right-wing and the national organization is left-wing. It is that the local union's view is local and narrow, in both space and time. It sees three hundred workers perhaps losing their jobs. It is unmoved by arguments that four and one-half million other American workers would not have jobs if their policies of protectionism were followed out to the hilt. Moreover, it cannot hold still to listen to arguments about what is good for its community and its workers five or ten years from now. It is preoccupied, and understandably so, with the prospect of three hundred unemployed union members in a particular local watch factory or glove factory or zinc mine or tuna fleet or bicycle factory—*right now*.

And so, in this typical situation, we are apt to see, not a class or party or left-right struggle, but a local employer, a local banker, a local labor leader, a petition signed by three hundred local workers, a local Democratic senator (with a very "liberal" reputation) and a local Republican congressman—all staunchly lined up in favor of high tariffs, quotas, protectionism, and sharp curtailment of foreign trade. Ranged on the other side, you will find employers, bankers, labor leaders, workers, Democratic senators and congressmen and Republican senators and congressmen (including some with a "conservative" reputation) all staunchly lined up in favor of freer trade, for the good of the country as a whole, and for the good of each part of the country in the long pull.

This basis of explaining polarization on the perennial tariff issue has been brought out in the open before now. Long ago, the cry of the protectionists was, "Tariff is a local issue." If they were right, and if nothing mattered except the immediate town-by-town and mill-by-mill gain or loss from a particular tariff action, it would be difficult to quarrel with the policies deduced from that premise. But if the sum total of individual tariff actions affects markedly the over-all prosperity and standard of living of a people, and even their prospects for collective security and peace, then an entirely different set of conclusions follows.

And the key to it all has almost no relation to left-right, Communist-Fascist, liberal-conservative gradations; the key to it all is broad, long-term, public-interest, nationwide, even worldwide appraisal of advantage, as against narrow, short-term, parochial, local-interest, special-interest, or group-interest appraisal of advantage.

Labor Relations as a Broad-Narrow Problem

Since attitudes by and toward labor figure very prominently in any assessment of political classification, labor issues form an excellent test of our new yardstick.

Extremely low wages might, for a particular employer and for a temporary period, show a profit and appear to be an advantageous labor policy. But for the country's economy as a whole, and for the long pull, good wages are good business.

Conversely, a policy on the part of unions or workers of taking every advantage of the employer and doing as little work as possible might, in some local plant and for a brief time, seem to an extremist or irresponsible union to serve its interests. But for the labor movement as a whole and workers as a whole, and certainly for the country as a whole and for the long pull, this sort of thing is self-defeating.

A little earlier in this chapter it was said that, on the new scale, extremists of both the conventional Right and the conventional Left would be found grouped at one end—the narrow. The labor issues illustrates how this works out.

The extreme right-wing idea of keeping wages as low as possible, resisting all improvements in social insurance, and fighting the growth of unionism at every step is clearly a narrow view in terms of interest and time. As we have seen, good wages, good social insurance, and healthy labor organization are all beneficial to the country as a whole and the economy as a whole, and therefore also to any particular employer in the long run.

The extreme left-wing idea of wringing out of the employer anything that labor has the *de facto* power to wring out of him, then giving in return as little labor as possible, and, indeed, using the power of labor if possible to bring the employer to his knees and perhaps take over his prerogatives—all this is obviously not good for the country, for the economy, or for labor as a whole, or for anyone over a long period.

The labor issue also highlights how the broad-narrow test follows logically when you abandon the class-struggle doctrine and substitute the mutual-interest doctrine as a starting point.

The broader your point of view and mental grasp are, the more clearly you see the mutual interest of business and labor.

The narrower your point of view and mental grasp are, the more the political-economic scene will present itself to your mind as a class struggle. For you see only your own immediate gains and your supposed adversary's losses.

It is no mere coincidence, then, that Communists and Fascists seem to have so much in common, and that extreme right-wing employers and extreme left-wing labor spokesmen unconsciously talk the same language and use the same assumptions. They all assume the class struggle. They just happen to be on different sides of it.

Indeed, if the extreme right-wing employers had had things their way, they would have acted out the scenario of history exactly as it was written out for them by Marx, dutifully playing their parts and mouthing their lines. Thus they would have been improving the chances that the Marxian prediction would be fulfilled.

It was not adverse interest that wrecked the Marxian scenario; it was mutual interest. And mutual interest was possible because enough people took a society-wide, decades-long view of events and advantages.

Government Regulation as a Broad-Narrow Problem

The old-fashioned Right used to oppose any government regulation of business whatever. The old-fashioned Left, at the extreme, favored a complete take-over of business by government.

Again, both positions are narrow in concept.

As shown earlier, modern industry and commerce could not exist except within a framework of government licensing, inspection, and umpiring. Any businessman who cannot see this truth has blinders that are close-fitting indeed. If his narrow view prevailed, our economy would still be primitive and our standard of living only a fraction of what it is.

Equally narrow is the view that cannot see that excessive governmental involvement would have been, if anything, more deadly, and would have snuffed out the essential spark of incentive, risk, and freedom that has exploded the energies of this country with such tremendous results.

Both views are narrow simply because they refuse to see the essential contribution that government, on the one hand, and private enterprise, on the other, are capable of making to the long-term, countrywide prosperity of

60

the people if government and business are both accepted as good rather than evil forces.

A good example under this general heading is the matter of monopoly and restraint of trade.

The old-fashioned view of big business, fixing its narrow sights solely upon the grossly obvious gain of acquiring more and more complete control over the market, was presumably to let the growth of monopoly run its natural course without government interference. To the interested adventurers, it might seem too plain for argument that their interests would be served by cornering the market and then sitting back, free of competition, to exact fat prices and profits from a helpless public.

But would this best serve the interests of free private enterprise as a whole? Nowadays the answer to this question is also too plain for argument. We know that if one sector after another of a private-enterprise economy is taken over by a monopoly, this would eventually mean the death of free enterprise. We have observed the history of the cartels of Europe. We have seen their stultifying effect on technical progress and their stagnating effect on expansion of trade in good products at low prices. And we have seen how monopoly paves the way for nationalization and Fascism, since the economy is laid out on a platter in convenient parcels to be taken over by any strong-armed dictator of either "Left" or "Right."

Fortunately, instinctive good sense led to the passage about three-quarters of a century ago of the Sherman Antitrust Act. The policy of that Act evidenced an intuitive realization of the paradoxical truth that free enterprise, to remain free, could not be completely free. Some of the inherent forces of free business could, under certain conditions, lead progressively to monopoly. The bigger a business got, the stronger its competitive position might become; the less it would be subject to business cycles; the more it could invest in experimentation and product improvement; the less it would be dependent on outside capital; the more it could drive down the cost of what it bought by quantity bargaining; the more it could cut its profit margins and undersell its remaining competitors. Then, if a hands-off government conveniently looked the other way, it could assert some rougher advantages. It could selectively undersell one competitor at a time in successive areas, by selling at a loss. It could bully suppliers out of supplying competitors. It could buy up patents and processes and keep them away from competitors. And so on—the devices are endless and familiar.

All of this could happen if free enterprise were free in the absolute sense.

Free enterprise, left completely to itself, might thus destroy its own freedom. And so the extreme proponents of untrammeled business freedom would appear in the end as its worst enemies.

Most modern businessmen, including practically all "big" businessmen, now realize this. You see evidence of it when, for example, you learn that Ford and General Motors are genuinely worried over the prospect that Packard or Nash or Hudson or Studebaker might succumb. In older, less discerning times, the biggest auto manufacturer might have slavered eagerly over the juicy prospect of cutting down Packard, Nash, Hudson, and Studebaker one by one, with delicious deliberation, by well-timed price wars, financial onslaughts, and threats to suppliers. Instead, the bigger corporations now hover with furrowed brows over the statistics of relative sales, hoping that the smaller company sales will not sink below that line which means the end of one more competitor.

To say that free enterprise, left completely to itself, might destroy its own freedom is not to detract in the slightest from its value as unquestionably the most potent organism of prosperity the world has ever known. It is only to say that power without restraint is ineffectual and self-defeating.

If one may adapt an illustration of André Gide's, which he used in another connection: Turn a kite loose in a high wind—it will not rise unless it is restrained by a string. So restrained, it enjoys the freedom of flight high above the earth. But without restraint it falls and is earthbound.

So it is with free enterprise. It rises and soars because of the restraints placed upon its raw force by such governmental measures as the antimonopoly laws. For these restraints, in turn, bring out and enhance its inner operating principle, which is active competition.

Here again, it may be pointed out that the extremists are clustered together at the same end. Just as both Communists and Fascists have usually been against free international trade and have stressed internal self-sufficiency, and just as both Communists and Fascists have accepted the class struggle and sought to act out rather than discredit the Marxian blueprint, so also both Communists and Fascists have favored monopoly, by state or by cartel, as against the preservation of free competition.

The Farm Issue as a Broad-Narrow Problem

The side-taking on the farm issue provides an almost perfect illustration of how the broad-narrow cleavage rules our controversies rather than the left-right cleavage.

On the side of high, rigid farm price supports are ranged those who are preoccupied with (a) maintaining farm prices *this year,* with (b) the interests of one particular group, the farmers, and with (c) only the financial interests of that group.

On the side of gradual replacement of rigid price supports by natural market conditions are those who are concerned with (a) getting farm prices on a healthy self-sustaining basis year in and year out, with (b) the interests not only of the farmer but of the consumer, and of the economy as a whole, and with (c) not merely the farmer's financial interest, but his interest as a human being in self-respect and freedom from exasperating controls.

The record since World War II demonstrates that rigid price supports, while they may sometimes hold up farm income temporarily, stimulate the increase of the very crop surpluses that depress farm prices. And so, the only cure for the evils created by price supports becomes more price supports, which in turn produce more surpluses.

The government carries on a valiant struggle to dispose of these surpluses. With the degree of price support flexibility that has been won in recent years, some substantial successes have been achieved in this process in some commodities. But it is plain that if the high rigid supports were continuously in effect, the struggle would be a hopeless one. The only outcome would be the piling up in the future of surpluses so staggering that they would burst all bounds of disposal and perhaps even of storage.

By contrast, the record also shows that where price supports have been gradually and flexibly adjusted to permit free market forces to exert themselves more fully, farm prices have slowly but surely gone up.

It must be stressed that the alignment here is not one group against another. It is not the farmers against everyone else. It is the farmers, organizations, and politicians with the long broad view versus farmers, organizations, and politicians with the short narrow view.

The broad view consists partly in giving weight to factors other than those of financial return. An increasing number of farmers prefer to take their chances financially, if they can only increase their freedom from crop and acreage controls, inspections, reports, and red tape. It is not merely the time-consuming nuisance of these controls. It is also the nagging presence of continuing restraints on personal independence of judgment and action.

The farmer, after all, likes to think of himself as the prototype of the individualist, the free man. Traditionally, and by the nature of his work and his environment, he tends to rely on his own resources and judgment. He does not stand at an assembly line, or work on a construction crew, or share in the coordinated tasks of some large office force. Rather, he rides his tractor through his fields in solitude. Often he cannot see another human being from one horizon to the other. He sizes up the weather, the markets, and the soil, and decides for himself what, where, and when to plant, cultivate, harvest, and sell. He is forced to cope personally with emergencies—a broken implement, a sick cow, a fire, a sudden freeze or hailstorm.

This, then, is not a man who is going to run with a herd into a "left-wing" position of abdicating all his problems—and his rights of choice—to the government.

Under the old scale of left and right, government takeover of responsibility and power in business (including the farm business) is the hallmark of leftism. Anyone who accepts this old scale, and who assumes that the government-control, government-subsidy system is the future of American farming, is thus in effect saying that American farmers are a mass of left-wingers, and can be counted on to behave as such. Political calculations made on this assumption are bound to be exploded in time. The preposterousness of this assumption merely forms one more evidence of the impossibility of analyzing American politics in left-right terms.

The Issue of Veterans' Rights as a Broad-Narrow Problem

There is a curious parallel between the farm issue and the issue of veterans' rights.

For, just as some spokesmen for our ruggedest rugged individuals, the farmers, seem most determined to perpetuate and increase statist control of the individual in the farm economy, so some spokesmen for our most "anti" antisocialists, the veterans' organizations, seem most determined to socialize health services in the United States.

The way this comes about is as follows: Because of the wide incidence of military service in World War II and the years following, and because of the availability of many benefits to families of veterans, we are approaching the point where a very large fraction of our population will be veterans, or within the embrace of veterans'-benefit systems. Therefore, if governmental hospital and medical services for non-service illnesses for veterans and their families were to accumulate into the future, the result would be about as close to socialization of a major segment of American medicine as anyone could expect to see.

This is far from being mere speculation and theory. We

like to emphasize that our social legislation system contains nothing resembling British "socialized medicine." We rejected a plan for nationalized health services after an extended and sometimes heated debate. Yet one wonders how many of the people who view the British system with alarm realize that the United States actually operates a larger "socialized" hospital system than Britain does. Our veterans' hospital system is the largest on earth.

Reduced to the broad-narrow mensuration: Those who look only at the personal advantage to one group, and at the present advantage exclusively, will continue to press for maximum government benefits, insurances, pensions, medical and hospital services to veterans and their families as a class apart; those who look at the impact on the country as a whole for the long term, and see the mounting threat to our traditions and institutions of private health services, will take their stand in favor of gradual obliteration of the line between veteran and non-veteran, except as to privileges and obligations reasonably related to military service.

Middle-of-the-Road "Extremists"

One of the interesting by-products of the broad-narrow index is the way in which it throws a new light on at least

69

some of the people who have in the past been called "middle-of-the-roaders."

It has been mentioned that, on this new scale, extremists of both the Left and the Right are found huddled together at the "narrow" terminal, and at the opposite terminal will be found many, if not most, of the more active middle-of-the-roaders.

Of course, there are many varieties of middle-of-the-roader. There are those who are so classified by default, since they do not have enough convictions to put them anywhere else. And there are those who are so classified because they diversify their views to hedge their political bets.

But a large number of people whose views and actions are classed as "center" are people who are trying to give full effect and credit to all the major forces of national and international life, in such a way that their capacity to serve and support each other will indeed be brought out.

Once this is accepted it gives a new look to these "middle-of-the-roaders." In the past, they have sometimes been thought of as sort of milk-and-water compromisers, without much imagination or courage or excitement about them.

By contrast, the crusading, starry-eyed "left-winger" or the anti-crusading, steely-eyed "right-winger" somehow appeared, if wrong, at least romantic.

People wrote plays about idealistic "left-wing" professors or reporters combating, and always defeating, formidable "right-wing" college trustees or scrap dealers. But no one ever wrote plays about middle-of-the-roaders. At last a play did appear, *The Egghead*, by Molly Kazan, in which the "left-wing" professor refreshingly proved to be wrong and the common-sense people around him right —but the play had only a short run.

Yet, an extreme "leftist" or "rightist" seldom needs to think. The direction of his opinion and his pressure is fixed in advance. And so he doesn't deliberate, or weigh, or define, or select. He just pushes.

If his goal is wages, or profits, or governmental power, or labor power, or business power—he has only one motto: "More." This keeps his life simple, his days active, and his mind serene.

Never does he toss sleeplessly at night wondering whether he made the right choice on a close decision.

He is constantly under violent attack, but this bothers him not at all, for it comes only from one direction—the opposite extreme wing. And, since he has complete contempt for the opinions of his attackers, their shafts never pierce him. All this gives him a reputation as a dashing, courageous fellow. He has never known the suffering of the man who, no matter what decision he makes, is invariably attacked from *both* sides. He cannot understand this kind of suffering, because he does not realize that this man frequently has genuine respect for the opinion of many of his attackers, and is tortured by the thought that at least some of his attackers may be right.

Moreover, the "left-wing" or "right-wing" extremist always has the solace of a herd of identically-minded associates who will rally round him, reassure him, dress his wounds, and join him in comfortably well-established patterns of ridicule and wit at the expense of the opposition. He also has the comfort of having an obvious enemy, whom he can hate and contemn with joyous abandon. He knows nothing of the loneliness of the conscientious "middle-of-the-roader," painfully picking his way through a maze of issues, trying to decide each one right on its merits, and never quite knowing who is with him or what friend he might lose at each step of the way.

It is only because of the phony left-right scale that we ever could have failed to see that the one-way, one-track, narrow-gauge dogmas of either the extreme right or the extreme left really require little courage, less sensitivity, and still less discriminating intelligence.

But once we adopt a valid scale, we discover that the "extremism" of some "middle-of-the-roaders," which consists of taking the broadest possible view of public issues, and thereby bringing into balance the worldwide and century-long best interests of an entire people, requires much more thoughtfulness, imagination, generosity of spirit, and political courage than the extremism of the "far-leftists" and "far-rightists."

The Significance of the New Scale for American Democracy

Five examples have been given to indicate how the broad-narrow scale helps to explain the enigma of American politics in a way that the left-right scale cannot do: reciprocal trade, labor relations, government regulation, agriculture, and veterans' rights. Other examples could be added from both current affairs and American history. Of course, because of its geographical expanse, its multitude of local interests, its federal system, and its system of congressional representation by states and population, the United States would naturally have a greater inclination to develop this kind of pattern than a more compact and homogeneous country.

The direction and tone of American policy, both foreign and domestic, has depended on the extent to which the narrow-view or the broad-view people have achieved ascendancy.

This means that usually the antidote or counter to one narrow-view group is *not* some other narrow-view group. It usually has to be the broad-view group.

The reason is that narrow-view groups can only prevail by logrolling and *quid pro quo* deals. A farm bloc or silver bloc or veterans' bloc or billboard bloc can say to the others, "You support me, and I'll support you." Since, by definition, each is more interested in his narrow advantage than in the over-all public good, such deals are not uncommon, even among blocs that are completely unrelated and occasionally even incompatible by conventional standards. Thus, during the 1958 congressional session the farm bloc was letting it be known that unless the Administration supported their rigid price-support proposals they would cause trouble for the President on the reciprocal trade bill, on which they knew the President placed the very highest importance. Now, farm products are probably the largest single beneficiary of reciprocal trade legislation. Yet this particular group had its sights so narrowed that it was apparently willing to barter away the farmers' own interests on another front to get the farm bill passed that was immediately under their noses.

The lesson for American democracy is plain.

If American democracy ever goes down in failure, it will not be because it has been subverted by the Left, or corrupted by the Right, or caught in a smashup between the two.

It will be because the cumulative total strength of narrow interests has succeeded in surpassing the countervailing strength of broad, long-range public interest within the decision-making structure of the government. An example will show how this could happen.

Let us suppose that each congressman and each senator votes on the reciprocal trade issue on the strength of the short-range effect on a few businesses within his district, rather than on the long-range public interest. Certainly there are more than enough districts having some interests that are locally felt to be threatened by imports to produce a comfortable majority in both houses for a bill restricting imports.

Let us suppose that this cumulation of specific local impingements results in the initiation of a policy of higher and higher walls against imports. It would not be long before no one abroad had dollars with which to buy our exports. The results would be, domestically, that the four and one-half million Americans whose jobs depend on foreign trade would be in danger of unemployment. But worse, a chain reaction would be set in motion which would include retaliatory trade restrictions against us, a rash of protectionism and increased nationalism, severe damage to the newly-established European trade community idea, and finally a moving-in by the U. S. S. R. and Communist China to take over the trade relations we had thrown away, perhaps following their economic penetration with political penetration. It is no exaggeration to say that a single wrong action on such a measure as the reciprocal trade bill could be the beginning of disaster for the United States. And the sobering worry is that this kind of wrong action could conceivably come about, not because a majority of our people willed it so on the strength of the public interest involved, but because a majority against the over-all will of the people was pieced together by adding end-to-end a lot of separate local interests each one of which was comparatively minor and irrelevant to the great final issue of national and world prosperity and peace.

Similarly, if the United States ever loses its democratic private enterprise system, it will not lose it in a revolution of either the right or left, nor even as the result of "creeping socialism." The loss will come about as the result, again, of narrow-interest groups each succeeding in carving out of the democratic, free-enterprise total a segment of government subsidy, protection, and privilege. If the narrow group have their way on the farm and veterans' fronts, for example, we shall have, for a start, an ultimate loss of the independent status of agriculture and a huge chunk carved out of independent medicine. Increased subsidies of the merchant fleet, increased subsidies of certain primary metals, government take-over of hydroelectric power and eventually of commercial atomic power—all these things would occur if particular narrow-view groups prevailed. In time, the cumulative total of results would begin to approach genuine statism. The reason—and this is the central point of this discussion—would not be that left-wingers got their way, but that a succession of narrow-view selfish interests got their way, all the time swearing undying enmity toward "creeping socialism."

This particular phenomenon was not especially dangerous a century ago, when the effect of any mistakes flowing from excessive narrowness could not approach disaster proportions. But today this phenomenon is serious. The reason is that American policy has repercussions in every corner of the world, and many even hold the key to the fate of the planet Earth. *It follows that we cannot afford to have our foreign policy dictated by the cumulative pressure of unrelated local interests.*

Our foreign policy, and our domestic policy as well, must be based upon arguments and interests relevant to and proportionate to the epoch-making consequences of national decisions.

How do we ensure this? Must we change the structure of our representative government? Certain changes making for greater continuity and tenure, such as longer terms of office, might help. But changing the basis of representation is not the answer.

The only solution is the conscious assumption by all government officials, both legislative and executive, of a responsibility for the over-all long-range public good. We have been debating since the birth of our country whether the elected representative's primary duty is to forward the specific interests of his constituents as they see them, or the highest interest of the country and the world as he sees it. In almost every one of the vignettes of courage presented in Senator Kennedy's *Profiles in Courage,* this was the issue. And courage invariably took the form of serving the higher interest at the risk of local reprisals.

The point has been debated long enough. As the judges say, there must be an end of argument. Moreover, our new world responsibility introduces a new and crushingly conclusive weight into the scales. Government representatives and servants must serve the higher public interest first, or American democracy is doomed, and the world with it.

Foreign Policy as a Broad-Narrow Problem

The broad-narrow concept provides a clue, not only to alignments on American domestic issues, but also to the almost unique character of American foreign policy.

American foreign policy is of unprecedented breadth, in the sense that it attempts to give full credit to the legitimate national aims of every country in the world. This means that it frequently finds itself on *both* sides of international disputes, throwing its weight on the side not of unconditional victory by one side over the other, but of peaceful resolution of the dispute in such a way as to give the fullest possible recognition to the rights of both countries. Other countries, like England, have approached this posture, but never on quite so complete a scale.

By contrast, Soviet foreign policy is narrow. The Soviet Union can usually without thinking twice decide which side of any controversy it is on, and then uninhibitedly push that side's interests.

A few examples will show the difference.

In the Algerian dispute, we find our oldest ally, France,

on the one side. On the other we find the cause of Arab nationalism and independence.

As a practical matter, it is imperative that we maintain our traditional friendship with France. France lies at the heart of many solutions of the problems of Europe, including NATO and the various economic unions such as the Common Market and Euratom.

As a practical matter, it is equally imperative that we retain our friendly relations with the Arab countries, since the loss of the Middle East and North Africa would also have serious consequences of both a military and economic kind.

The Soviets are under no such restraints. They can go flat-out for Algerian nationalism. They have no objection whatever to alienating the French.

In the Kashmir dispute, we try to respect the claims of our friend Pakistan and of our friend India. The Soviets do not regard Pakistan—a Baghdad Pact country—as a friend, and can therefore again take sides with ease.

In the Gulf of Aqaba dispute, we have on the one side the Israeli case for freedom of navigation, which has a strong appeal. But on the other side we have the passionate determination of Saudi Arabia, another of our friends, that for religious and other reasons its control of those straits shall be recognized. To destroy our friendship with Saudi Arabia at a time like this is unthinkable.

The narrow Soviet position is again an easy one. It is simply anti-Israel, and that is that.

The two main differences between the Soviet approach and ours are these: First, we strive to help the emerging countries and peoples of the world into economic and political maturity and self-reliance; the Soviets, as Lenin plainly indicated in his famous 1924 speech, seek to achieve the dominance of international Communism by ultimately extending satellite status to other countries and colonies, under cover of encouraging nationalism and anti-imperialism. Second, we are determined that the transformations and adjustments that are going on around the world take place with a minimum of violence; the Communists are quite willing to employ and encourage violence as an instrument of policy.

Now, there is an important moral to be drawn from this distinction, which neither Americans nor their friends should forget in the troubled times in which we live. When critics conclude that our foreign policy seems to suffer repeated setbacks, while Soviet foreign policy seems to score repeated successes, let them remember the enormous difference in difficulty between the foreign-policy problem of the Soviets and the foreign-policy problem of the United States. Then let the apparent successes or failures be judged in relation to the difficulty of the assignment.

It is all too easy to look at the Kashmir or Aqaba or Algerian tangles and conclude that the Soviet policy-makers are possessed of uncanny diabolical cleverness, while our own policy-makers are inept and indecisive. Yet, one cannot help feeling that, given the Soviet aims and presumptions, it is a relatively simple matter to contrive the Soviet foreign policy line in these situations. But to devise and administer exactly the right line from the United States' point of view, to achieve a maximum of progress with a minimum of violence—this takes far more wit, skill, and patience.

There is a close parallel here with the relative difficulty, already discussed, of being an advocate of a narrow point of view on a domestic issue, and of taking the broad view which gives due credit to the merits of both sides.

Any dim-witted demagogue could go into a town where race problems were causing tensions and inflame these tensions into violence. Indeed, several have done so before now. But it takes the highest kind of wisdom and skill to bring about real progress in race relations, steadily, decisively, and also peacefully.

The same disparity in difficulty confronts us, not only

in relation to disputes between foreign countries, but in relation to conflicts between groups within foreign countries.

In the countries of Asia, Africa, and Latin America, the most significant single group to emerge in modern times is the new educated class of students, teachers, intellectuals, professional people, labor leaders, and salaried public and private managers. Over and over again we see a pattern of conflict emerging: the new educated class versus the rulers—whether the rulers are aristocrats, dictators, or both.

You will find that many of these students and intellectuals got their education in the United States, have strong ties with the United States, and, indeed, acquired their burning desire for more freedom and more progress by having had a taste of freedom and progress in the United States. Yet these very intellectuals are apt to turn up as the bitterest enemies of the regime in their own home countries. When the regime happens to be officially friendly to the United States, this once more puts our foreign policy under severe strain from two sides.

The writer once sat up all night in Baghdad with seven young Iraqi professional men, who personified this problem as it appears throughout Asia, Africa, and Latin America. Every one of them had been educated in America. Every one of them had only the highest admiration for American ideals and methods and accomplishments. Yet every one of them was violently opposed to the pro-American government of Nuri as-Said. Why? Because under Nuri's sometimes heavy hand, they did not enjoy the kind of freedom and personal opportunity they had come to know in the United States. Moreover, by a sort of reflex action, they idolized Colonel Nasser. It was useless to point out that, when it came to being heavy-handed with the home folks, Nasser could probably give lessons to Nuri, and that if they lived in Egypt they would probably be even more restive than they were in Iraq. And it was useless to argue that freedoms of the kind they found in America cannot be created overnight in a country like Iraq, and that therefore they should not judge Nuri's methods by the standards of Jefferson. They can admit these arguments to their minds, but their hearts are in a hurry.

The riots in Latin America during Vice-President Nixon's 1958 trip were due to the counterpart of this situation, probably more than to any other single cause. The hottest issue in these countries was revulsion against local dictators. The intellectuals were in the vanguard of this fight, which was increasingly producing results, by breaking the traditional grip of the social and economic aristocracy on government and replacing the traditional ruling groups with representatives of the new educated class.

Now, by a process that contained much emotion but little logic, these intellectuals had identified the United States with the hated dictators. Why? Because the United States had recognized the dictators and dealt with them as an officially friendly government, all under our policy of noninterference in the internal affairs of other countries. Of course, if we ever abandoned that policy and proceeded to use our power to bring down governments we disapproved of and create governments more to our liking, the screams of anti-American protest from the same countries would make the 1958 shouts sound like the voice of the turtle dove in spring.

Once more, see how relatively easy the Soviet assignment is. They do not mind interference in the internal affairs of free countries. Indeed that is the heart and soul of the program of international Communism. And they do not mind violence.

As the new educated class begins to put its own governments into power, it will undoubtedly begin to understand a truth which is crucial to their future. When you are a dissident group seeking to dislodge an existing regime, both outside interference and violence may look attractive. But when you are yourself in the position of responsibility, the traditional American policy of nonviolence and respect for the right of people to choose their own government will begin to be seen for what it is—the only possible policy which can combine peace and progress in a world in transition.

And, as education, communication, and exchanges grow and improve, the members of the new educated class in all these countries, and the people of the United States, will more and more realize what a strong tie of common interest, thought, and purpose binds them together.

The tragedy is that this realization has been too slow in coming to prevent such episodes as the attacks on Vice-President Nixon in South America and the strains associated with the *coup d'état* in Iraq. Just as the Latin American intellectuals wrongly insist on identifying us with their dictators, so the Arab intellectuals tenaciously cling to the mistaken idea that America is actively opposed to their dream of Pan-Arabism. This is in spite of such statements as the following, from President Eisenhower's letter of July 22, 1958, to Chairman Khrushchev:

This does not mean that the United States is dedicated to a perpetuation of the *status quo* in the Arab world. The United States recognizes and sympathizes with the yearning of the

Arab peoples for a greater nationalistic unity. For example, the United States promptly recognized the United Arab Republic, bringing together Egypt and Syria, as soon as it was apparent that the change was accepted by the people concerned and after the new government had undertaken to meet the normally applied international standards.

Here, then, is a place where the need is especially acute for stressing our over-all theme: that what we are for will support and advance the legitimate aspirations of other countries.

Our overriding concern from now on, particularly in Asia, Africa, and Latin America, must be to get closer to this new educated class, learn what their hopes and plans for their people are, help them accommodate those hopes and plans to the realities of today's world, and above all reach a state of affairs in which they and we are where our common convictions ought to place us: on the same side!

The "narrow" approach to international issues is, of course, by no means confined to Communist states. It is only natural that many of the countries of the world will be found to be preoccupied with a vigorously partisan view on a limited range of issues.

Colonel Nasser dissolves all international issues in the one solvent of how they fit in with his ambitions for a

Pan-Arab nation. Chiang Kai-shek sees world questions in relation to his dream of regaining the mainland of China. And so on and on around the globe.

Certainly we must try to understand all these specific preoccupations. But, in return, we are also entitled to hope that the individual nations will make an effort to understand the problem of the United States which is trying to do justice to the valid aspirations of all peoples, to resist highhanded and arbitrary interference with national and personal freedoms from any source, and to do all this while preserving a basically harmonious world.

Chapter
FOUR

Human Nature and Ideology

So far, in summarizing what we are for, we have concentrated mostly on the currently-crucial issue of the relation of government to the economy and to people, in a modern industrial or industrializing society.

This, of course, is only part of the portrait of what we are for. There are many other parts that must be added to make the picture complete. They have to do with such principles as freedom, property, incentive, competition, justice, individuality, national pride, and religion.

However, our need for a statement of what we are for is not met, either for our own use or for achieving understanding overseas, by offering a Sears, Roebuck catalogue of virtues. What we need is a unifying, pervading principle, which catches up in one lucid theme the essence of all these virtues.

The unifying principle is this:

Human beings have certain common basic motivations, drives, needs, and aspirations. What we stand for, and what we seek for people all over the world, is in direct and natural line with these basic motivations, drives, needs, and aspirations. What totalitarian Communism stands for is in direct and artificial defiance of these basic characteristics of human nature.

It will be observed that this principle is well suited for the overseas use to which it should be put: that of *identification*.

It is not very useful or effective to state what we are for in the abstract, or as an exercise in debaters' tactics, or as a take-it-or-leave-it proposition. Too many attempts at this kind of statement seem to assume that the world idea struggle will be won in some kind of gigantic global debating hall, and that our success will depend on the ability of Americans to hold their own through facile and documented point-by-point exposition of the merits of the American case. It is true that there are occasions when the inability of Americans to do justice to their own cause in direct controversy is embarrassing or worse.

Examples range all the way from the poor showing made by some of our prisoners when subjected to skillful ideological brainwashing in Korean War prison camps, to the discomfiture of American tourists caught in the smart banter of Parisian café-table political talk.

It would help greatly if we could all turn in a better performance on all such occasions; but this is not quite the way the idea contest is going to be won or lost.

We shall not win, in other words, by tackling the fellow who has taken up a position on the opposite side of the ideological argument, and skillfully putting him to rout by the cogency and splendor of our dialectic performance.

We shall "win" by making it plain to the people of the world that we and they are not on opposite sides, but rather that we are, as fellow human beings, essentially striving for the same things, and that what we are for will help them to achieve the legitimate progress they are striving for.

With identification rather than disputation as our watchword, then, let us review several of the fundamental motivations of human beings and see whether our principle is valid. In so doing, we must not be put off by the well-known fact that exceptions to almost any trait of human nature can be found. The characteristics here listed are, for the most part, so widespread and so ingrained that they can safely be called normal features of human nature.

Freedom

The urge to be free is one of the innate, bred-in-the-bone traits of human nature.

Take a child a month old. Hold its arms and legs so that they cannot be moved. The child will scream its head off.

Not because you are hurting it. The restraint may be as gentle and affectionate as you please. But because you are violating one of its deepest human needs—the need to be free.

This is not something that the child learns in school, or has conferred upon it by the government. It is not something acquired by reading Rousseau or Paine or the Bill of Rights. It is unlearned and intrinsic.

This truth is not diminished by the fact that some people have for a time been made to tolerate lack of freedom, when they appear to have no alternative. We are not here concerned with what abnormal shapes the human spirit can be molded into if the heat and pressure are severe enough. We are concerned with the normal shape of the human spirit—for it is into that shape the spirit will spring when given any kind of choice.

We might as well face the fact, when making arrangements about society, that this is the kind of creature *homo sapiens* is. There are some creatures that do not possess this compulsion to be free. But man is not a Guernsey cow or a drone bee or a sea anemone.

Why is imprisonment one of the commonest forms of human punishment? The prisoner gets food, shelter, leisure, and the highest known standard of security. In fact, the standard of living is frequently higher than that which he previously enjoyed. Yet the loss of freedom not only offsets all this but converts the condition into one of severe punishment.

Why is it that, throughout history, millions of people have fought hundreds of battles, large and small, for national and personal freedom? And why have men repeatedly gone to their deaths rather than give up freedom to speak out on politics or laws or religion? Why didn't they just go home and relax?

It is because man is that kind of creature, and cannot help it.

There was a period, during which we heard much of the sinister technique of mass brainwashing, when we began to wonder whether entire generations could not be turned into robots whose urge to freedom was as thoroughly ground out of them as the fight is bred out of a pet lamb. But the Hungarian uprising revised all calculations on that score. Here was a revolt, initiated and executed largely by members of that very generation, who supposedly had heard almost nothing except skillful Communist propaganda since they were old enough to be interested in political affairs. Yet they spontaneously erupted one day in a largely unplanned assault on those whose essential offense was an offense against freedom. Revised calculations about the Eastern European countries now have to assume that, instead of containing a placid drove of robots with scientifically-controlled wills, they contain a tightly-coiled steel spring called the urge to be free. This spring can remain coiled, without losing its lightning resilience, for not only years but generations. Let the restraining pressure weaken a little, and the spring will lash out just as it did in Hungary.

Even in the U. S. S. R. or Red China, we have seen how quickly people have responded to the slightest easing of controls on self-expression. As soon as there is even a hint that a little freedom of opinion might be tolerated, as in the post-Stalin era and in Mao's "let-a-hundred-flowers-bloom" period, there suddenly appear books, articles, wall newspapers, political commentaries—all springing up almost overnight, as if to prove that the habit of freedom had not become lost through disuse. The freedom has usually been short-lived and deceptive, but it has opened a crack in the surface long enough to reveal once more that under the crust of regimentation the urge of human freedom is still seething.

If, then, the urge to be free is fundamental in the human make-up, the ultimate rightness and success of a political arrangement will turn on whether it facilitates or frustrates that urge.

Enterprise democracy is intended to facilitate freedom, and does so in fact. Communism, by contrast, subordinates freedom to other goals, both in theory and in practice, with a few special exceptions which prove the rule, and which will be discussed later.

This being so, most American attempts to sum up what we are for have seized upon this one concept: freedom.

This is good and right. Why then does it not solve our problem merely to proclaim to the world: "We are for freedom"?

The principal reason is that the struggle actually centers around, not ideas in the abstract or philosophical sense, but ideas translated into institutions, laws, political structures, and economic systems.

The human spirit can achieve freedom in a subjective sense, of course, in defiance of almost any amount of anti-freedom environment. We can all think of men whose minds soared free while their bodies were locked in dungeons, and of artists whose creative imaginations ranged widely while their cold limbs were huddled in garrets, and of saints whose souls encompassed the universe while their earthly frames were confined to a cave or cell.

The mind of man has throughout history repeatedly and consistently formulated and asserted the principle of human freedom. The idea itself is not a recent invention, and certainly not an innovation of Western civilization. For forty centuries Oriental thought has worked upon this theme. The world's great religions, sprung from Oriental soil, have concerned themselves with the spiritual essence of man, which decisively raises him above the level of a chattel or animal to be owned and enslaved. Almost every area and every epoch has made its contribution to the unfolding concept of freedom.

And yet it is only recently, and only in a few places, that the institutional means of realizing and perpetuating human freedom have begun to take effective shape.

These institutional means are numerous, but in the last analysis they fall mostly under two headings: political and economic.

Assuming that we begin with an intellectual and religious foundation on which to build the structures of freedom, true freedom will rise in proportion to the amount of both political and economic freedom a country's institutions afford to the separate person.

By political freedom is here meant freedom which is exerted and guaranteed through the right to influence governmental actions and procedures. It begins with the right to govern one's self through elected representatives. From this right flow constitutions protecting freedom of press, speech, thought, and worship. The rule of law is established, and a legal system is evolved that impartially and on the merits vindicates the freedoms and rights of all men, great or small, toward each other, and toward the government. Free public education is afforded, which must stand behind any system of universal suffrage.

These and many other freedom-expressing institutions grow up and expand because individual persons have the political power to demand them.

But, throughout the history of the struggle for freedom, there has run a parallel strand: that of economic freedom.

There is a sort of chicken-and-egg causal problem here. One could say that individual persons have succeeded in wresting more political power only as they have established more economic power to back up the demand. Or one could say that, as men have obtained increased political rights, they have been able to bring about conditions in which their individual economic stature could progressively be increased. One thing is clear: The two will usually be found together. If one exists alone, it will either eventually disappear or be joined by the other.

The long debate, which has gone on practically ever since the concept of voting was originated, on whether the ownership of property should be a prerequisite to the right to vote, is an illuminating example of the parallelism followed by political and economic freedoms. This controversy was very prominent in the early history of America, as evidenced, for example, by the lifelong correspondence on the subject between Adams and Jefferson, and the thunderous debates at the New York Constitutional Convention.

Both sides seemed to agree on the central point, which was that in a democracy it was desirable that economic and political rights should coincide in the citizen's hands. The question was, should you wait until he had acquired his economic standing before entrusting him with political rights, or should you give him political rights in order to help him along the road toward greater economic rights? One way or another, under enterprise democracy, he has usually managed to get both.

Earlier the formula for tyranny was stated as:

$$T = E + P$$

or, Tyranny equals economic plus political power, in the hands of the government.

The corollary of that formula can now be stated. The formula for freedom in the individual is:

$$F = E' + P'$$

Individual freedom equals economic rights plus political rights.

A person could, at least hypothetically, be completely free economically and unfree politically. An example would be a wealthy man living under a despotic regime. He is unfettered by any cares about his material prosperity. But because his political and legal rights are subject to the will of an arbitrary ruler, there is always the possibility that the despot may one day chop off his head and seize his fortune.

More relevant in modern times, however, is the possibility of a man who is free politically but might be unfree economically. This is the man who has the right to vote, the protection of the courts, free education, and freedom of movement, speech, religion, and all the rest, but who is so poor that he has not the time nor the opportunity nor the facilities to live as a free being should. The wretched mill and mine workers of Britain a century ago had an impressive array of legal and political rights guaranteeing their freedom. But to the man, woman, or child

99

who had to work from before dawn until after dark every day in order to stay alive, it was obvious enough that political freedom did not of itself mean living the life of a free person.

The need for this broader concept of freedom was well brought out by President Eisenhower in his 1958 Law Day message. He first quoted the eloquent passage from Burke on the essence of the supremacy of law:

The poorest man may in his cottage bid defiance to all the forces of the Crown. It may be frail; its roof may shake; the wind may blow through it; the storms may enter, the rain may enter,—but the King of England cannot enter; all his forces dare not cross the threshold of that ruined tenement!

President Eisenhower then added:

True, it is good that the King cannot enter unbidden into the ruined cottage. But it is not good that men should live in ruined cottages. The law in our times also does its part to build a society in which the homes of workers will be invaded neither by the sovereign's troops *nor* by the storms and winds of insecurity and poverty.

It was political "freedom" without economic freedom that Marx ridiculed. Of course, what he meant by bourgeois freedom was absolutely unbridled free trade, free competition with no holds barred, and free exploitation of workers to any extent that economic power would allow. He concluded—and Communists ever since have concurred—that freedom should be subordinated to the necessity of creating the communist state.

The real story of the past century can be summarized as follows:

Marx looked at the capitalist world and concluded that workers could well afford to submit to a dictatorship of the proletariat in order to throw off what he considered their economic slavery. In the outcome, as exemplified by events in the Soviet Union, the workers lost both their political freedom and their economic freedom, and all political and economic power lodged solidly in the hands of a small ruling bureaucracy.

The capitalist world, meanwhile, deeply conscious of the economic unfreedom and insecurity of many of its workers, proceeded to evolve the system of enterprise democracy which, through good wages, strong unions, social insurance, and guaranteed bargaining rights, re- sulted in adding a high degree of economic freedom to the political freedom that already existed and continued to grow. In short, while the Marxian course brought both political and economic unfreedom, the enterprise democ- racy course brought both political and economic freedom.

But, one must hasten to add, this freedom is by no means as perfect and complete as it can and should be made. There is plenty of unfinished business on the agenda of freedom.

As to freedom then, in summary: It is less important to stress that we are for freedom (since most uncommitted peoples accept freedom as an ideal) than to stress that *we are for the institutions that in fact create and advance freedom.*

The structure of Communism has unfreedom built right into it, for it takes out of the individual's hands and places in the government's hands all economic and political power. This does not mean that no freedom at all can be detected in Communist regimes. It merely means that the individual has no freedoms he can enforce as of right, and therefore must accept with gratitude such crumbs of freedom as may be thrown to him by his rulers.

The structure of enterprise democracy has freedom built into it, for it places in the individual's hands a combination of economic and political power that enables him to enforce his own freedom as of right.

Property

A second familiar human trait is the sense of property. A child at an early stage realizes that the foot he sees at the other end of the crib is *his* foot. It is not much of a transition from this to the idea that the ball he has been given for Christmas or the wooden sword he has made is *his* ball or *his* sword.

Again, no one has to teach him this. In fact, the big problem is to teach him that property rights are not absolute and unlimited, and that he must use his ball and his sword with due regard for the property rights of others.

Of course, at different stages and in different places, men have worked out all kinds of complex modifications of rights in property. But lying behind it all, there is always the instinctive feeling of a man that he is entitled to the fruits of his own toil or enterprise or invention, and there is a natural impulse to fight if anyone tries to violate those rights.

We make this sense of property the beginning point of our economic system, with its corollaries of competition, natural rewards for effort, natural penalties for sloth, and the tremendous incentive that goes with the knowledge that you can possess the results of your exertions.

Communism begins by undermining the concept of private property, puts all economic power in the hands of the state, and then tries to invent all kinds of substitute incentives and satisfactions.

Now, Communism as we know it today does not, of

course, abolish completely the concept of private property, although there have been some schools of Communism that would have gone all the way. It does abolish private ownership in productive property, except, as we shall see later, where departures have been made out of necessity or expedience. And, if we stick to the pure ideology, it does aspire to a world in which the possessory nexus between effort and end product is severed by the maxim, "From each according to his ability, to each according to his need." For what this obviously means, if it means anything, is that once your needs have been provided for (presumably according to someone else's estimates of your needs) thereafter you have no right to anything you may make or invent or dig or grow. This maxim cannot be dismissed as forgotten and meaningless dogma. It was, for example, reaffirmed and elaborately analyzed by a leading Soviet economist, K. V. Ostrovityanov, in a 1958 report to the Soviet Academy of Sciences.

We are not here concerned with hair-splitting about just how absolute the abolition of property by Communism might be under various interpretations of Communist dogma and at various stages in the Soviets' alleged advance toward Utopia, The essential fact is that Communist theory flies in the face of the inherent human sense of the right to possess the fruits of one's efforts, and proposes to build a society and an economy upon the assumption that this motivation can be sublimated and other motivations made to take its place.

From Marx on down, the typical Communist planner has had a colossal and cavalier contempt for human nature. To him the whole disgusting history of the race merely proved that human nature was a pretty poor piece of work and man could no longer be left to carve out his own destiny by pursuing his ridiculous desires. Instead, man's salvation on earth must be found in contriving a collective society in which all these human traits were artificially bludgeoned out of sight and replaced by an entirely new set of motivations, standards, and patterns of behavior devised by a small group of arrogant intellectuals.

And, of course, Exhibit A in this set of human attributes that were to be somehow removed from human history by force was the impulse to possess and own.

It is obvious that fundamental human attributes such as the instincts for freedom, for property, for justice, and for individuality are all of a piece. You cannot tamper with any of them without damaging the others. It is not surprising, then, that when Marx and the other theoreticians once started to flout human characteristics they went right down the list and flouted practically all of them.

The relation, for example, between property and freedom has already been noted. True freedom cannot exist without economic freedom. And economic freedom cannot exist without the concept of property. It is no answer to this to say that in a Communist state the system sees to it that people are fed and clothed and housed, and that this is the equivalent of economic freedom. As long as the state provides these things, the state can also withhold them. The result is that property, far from being a source of freedom, becomes a noose around the neck of every individual which the state can tighten at any moment at its whim.

Justice

Another fundamental human characteristic is a sense of justice.

Most people know justice when they see it, without having to take a graduate degree in jurisprudence.

Look back to your own childhood, to the time when your father came home one night and punished you for starting a fight that in fact was started by your sister. Did any flame ever burn more hotly than the fire of outraged self-righteousness that you felt then? You at that moment experienced one of the most vivid and blinding of all passions: the sense of justice affronted.

Through all the batterings and contortions of life, that sense of justice never leaves us. From childhood through adulthood, we make judgments every day that draw upon nothing more than a deep-seated human feeling for what is just. Listen to a group of children ordering their own affairs among themselves. Note how frequently you hear, "That's not fair." Not fair?—on the basis of what? Some local code of laws? Not at all. The chances are twenty to one that the same situation that made an American child exclaim "That's not fair" in Kansas would make a Burmese child exclaim "That's not fair" in Rangoon.

Or observe a group of adults reacting to the day's news. A train has been wrecked. One of the first questions on everyone's lips is, "Whose fault was it?" We demand to know, so that we can go on to the next step and identify what justice demands in the situation.

The history of jurisprudence has, for the most part, been a struggle to institutionalize man's innate sense of justice. We admit many imperfections in the stage we have attained in this process; but the significant thing is that we place the highest kind of priority on the object of justice for the individual, and we are consciously bending every effort to come closer to that goal. We also see as one of the highest possible international goals the establishment of a genuine rule of law between nations.

Communism, by contrast, again consciously downgrades justice and makes it subsidiary to the ends of the state.

We are here dealing not with polemics and rhetoric but with the actual language of constitutions and codes, and with their everyday interpretation and application by courts.

In the criminal codes of the various Soviet Republics, ever since 1922, there has been a clause which allowed courts to punish persons for any act which the court finds to be "socially dangerous." No informed adult needs to be told that this clause has been liberally used from time to time. It is not necessary for outsiders to allege that injustice was the result. One dead Communist leader after another has been posthumously rehabilitated to the status of an innocent victim by the Soviets themselves.

The law remains unchanged, however. Now and then the Soviet law professors gather up their courage and call for a change in this kind of provision. They did so in 1934, only to see the purge trials of 1936 as the answer to their efforts. They did so again in 1958, and it remains to be seen whether they will have any greater success.

Not only is the crime of "socially dangerous" conduct undefined. Even the punishment is unspecified. The court is allowed to impose a sentence on the basis of any article of the code which the judge considers to be "analogous."

This is not the only code section of this kind. It is a punishable crime to engage in "counterrevolution," a term which is made to include all kinds of activities such as "the undermining of state industry, transport, trade, currency, or system of credit, or of the cooperative system, with counterrevolutionary intent, by utilizing the state institutions or enterprises concerned or by working against their normal activities."

Even the law professors are not attacking this clause, although many a hapless factory manager who did not meet his quota has found himself purged and punished as a counterrevolutionary.

The Communist version of right and wrong can also be found defined in the Soviets' own standard encyclopedia. Volume 30 of the Great Soviet Encyclopedia explains "Soviet Morality" by setting forth the following quotation from Lenin:

"We say: that is moral which serves the destruction of the old exploitative society and the uniting of all workers around the proletariat creating the new society of Communists."

The Encyclopedia goes on to say:

In our time the only scientific criterion of morality is the defense of the interests of the victory of Communism . . .

The brittle artificiality of Communist efforts to find a party-line replacement for simple justice sometimes becomes downright funny. A good example is the story told by David Hotham in the March 6, 1958, issue of *The Reporter*. He told of a university professor who had been accused by his students of beating his wife. The crime was treated not as one of physical brutality but as one of rightist deviation. The case was discussed by the public and the press, and the professor was found innocent. It was now the turn of the accusing students to be accused —of leftist deviation. Then, after more weeks of debate, it turned out that the one who really beat the wife was the professor's mother. Whereupon the professor's mother was accused of rightist deviation.

Mr. Hotham's informant, who had recounted all this with a straight face and with evident approval of each successive diagnosis of the crime, then explained:

You see, it is like this. For a man to beat his wife or for a mother to beat her daughter-in-law smacks of the old reactionary society we have abolished. Therefore these people are rightist deviationists. On the other hand, the false charges against the professor resulted from the excess zeal shown by the students in trying to correct these outdated practices. The students are therefore leftist deviationists. It is really quite simple.

And so, while ninety-nine people out of a hundred, upon being hit without provocation, will unhesitatingly brand the act as unjust in itself, the devious Communist mind continues to try to create an ethic in which a left to the jaw is wrong because it is a rightist deviation.

Once more, in the concept of justice, we are reminded that human nature is indivisible, and that you cannot amputate part of it without destroying the identity of the whole. Justice and ownership can no more be disentangled than ownership and freedom. Indeed, the classical definition of justice, that of Plato, is cast in the language of ownership:

"Justice is to render unto every man that which is his own."

If no rule of law stands between a man and the destruction of his freedom and the destruction of his property rights for the good of the state, then, in the showdown, there is no freedom, no property, and no justice.

Individuality

Members of the human species have a strong urge to achieve individuality.

Most people want to be recognized as separate, identifiable, and somewhat special persons.

In children, we see it in the lengths to which the young will go to attract attention to themselves. In older people, we see it in the drive to acquire some kind of distinction, however minor, that sets one apart from the crowd. The ultimate ideal is to be better at something than anyone else, even if it is only being the greatest expert on ecclesiastical history from 1644 to 1646, or having the largest collection of Uruguayan stamps in Knox County, Tennessee. Failing such professional attainments as these, one may perhaps, as a last resort, grow a beard.

Each human individual knows that he is disparate, original, and particular. He senses that he has capacities for growth and self-expression that at times seem boundless. His drive to unfold his own personality is as real as the drive of a bush to unfold its leaves. Both can be pruned, but the drive is still there.

The Communists have struggled against the grain of human individuality. Even if we concede, for the sake of argument, a sort of minimal welfarism as their benefi-

cent goal, what a deadly-dull leveling of human person-
alities into faceless masses they are willing to accept as
the price! Figure out how many calories the human organism needs to survive, and let each organism have that
much food; if some organisms must burn more calories
in contracting their muscles at daily tasks, allow those
organisms more fuel for their bodies, according to the
degree of their exertions. Calculate how many cubic feet
of housing room the organism can be sheltered in without
severe damage, and provide this much housing. Adjust
wages, rents, prices, and rations to carry out this pattern.
Encourage drab and uniform clothing, and enforce drab
and uniform opinions. Make "deviation" the most hideous of all crimes.

This is the way Communist purists would prefer to
construct their society. Of course, we all know that nail
polish and trapeze dresses have invaded Moscow lately.
But this only confirms the main point, which is that individuals will be individuals anywhere—even in Russia.
In fact, *especially* in Russia, given half a chance.

Of course, what is at stake here is something far more
important than nail polish. We have placed a high value
on individualism, not because we want to encourage ec-
centricity or exhibitionism, but because we have learned
from experience that the greatest gains in human growth,

113

both individual and collective, are possible only when the separate person is free to be himself, and follow where his mind and spirit lead him. We believe, in short, that a solitary Eugene O'Neill writes better plays than a collective Hollywood scenario conference.

Group Allegiance

A familiar human trait is loyalty to and pride in the group that claims a person's principal allegiance. The group varies in different times and cultures. It may be a family, a clan, a city-state. Right now, in most parts of the world, the nation is the entity around which these loyalties cluster. The newer the country, the more emphatic this nationalism is asserted—which is only natural. Where nationhood does not exist, or exists in a form unsatisfactory to many of the people, as in the Arab world, the drive toward national identity is one of the most formidable forces of our time.

The sophisticated may lament this, and urge us all to be world citizens. But in the imperfect world of today, we might as well face the fact that it is through the vehicle of the particular nation that most people are striving to achieve their political and economic objectives and assert their impulse toward group self-expression.

Leaving aside for the moment the tactical concessions

sometimes made by Communism, we must not forget that the central plan of Communism is the subordination of separate nations to the Moscow-dominated international Communist movement. The Russians have had some success in appearing to obliterate the national identity of the various Asian states incorporated into the U. S. S. R., as well as of the Baltic States. The Eastern European satellites still retain the shell of national identity without real national rights. And in the pulling and hauling between the Soviet Union and Yugoslavia we have a constant reminder of how naggingly intolerable to Moscow is integrity and national independence in a neighboring Communist country.

Our country, on the other hand, is historically and ideologically the spiritual home of all who emerge from colonial dependency into responsible nationhood. Today we stand at the side of dozens of nations, with economic, military, and technical aid, anxious to see them succeed and prosper.

Nationalism, carried to excess, like individualism carried to excess, can be dangerous. But healthy nationalism, like healthy individualism, is a constructive force capable of eliciting the best that is in a nation or a person. The kind of world envisioned by Americans is a world of self-reliant, self-respecting, separate countries, working

115

together in a world organization in which each nation is represented as a matter of right, and settling their disputes in a world court as a matter of course. The kind of world envisioned by international Communism is a world of amorphous populations without national identities, controlled from a central point, and lavishing all allegiance only upon worldwide Communism.

But the human impulse of group allegiance cannot be diffused successfully to this degree, for when it becomes diffused it becomes nothing.

Wave after wave of invaders have tried to make the Hungarians forget that they are Hungarians, and the Poles forget that they are Poles—and the only result has been to make them more fiery Hungarians and Poles than before. Better to accept this human trait and build upon it than to deplore it, try to stamp it out, and reap only frustration and bitterness.

Religion

Finally, an almost universal human trait is religious feeling. Doctrines and forms and practices may vary widely. But the religious impulse is there, and will seek some kind of expression. Our tradition is a religious one. Within our borders, we have almost every kind of religion. And we respect the religious rights of others.

But the Communists, by their own account, propose to eradicate religion to make room for their own quasi-religion of Communism, even though, with unbelievable cynicism, they sometimes go about posing as the champions of Buddhists or Moslems as it may serve their immediate purpose.

After all, the Eastern Hemisphere has been the seedbed of the world's higher religions. It is no wonder, then, that Communism, as it woos the people of Asia, currently wears its antireligion beneath a heavy disguise.

This should fool no one, however. The reason is not so much the fact that for a hundred years Communist spokesmen and leaders have denounced religion as the opium of the people. The principal reason is that Communism is intrinsically incompatible with religion.

Enterprise democracy is a political and economic philosophy. It does not attempt to invade those areas of the human spirit that are the province of religion.

Communism, however, is not satisfied to ordain man's political and economic convictions; it must also break into the inner temple of man's spiritual life, and drag forth from him all his capacity for worship and adoration. He must be made to worship, as Toynbee puts it, collective human power.

Democracy and religion can exist side by side—indeed

are in alliance with each other; but Communism and religion cannot exist side by side in the same country, except as a temporary concession. This is true of all of the higher religions, for, as Toynbee says, they all agree on

. . . the conviction that Man is not the greatest spiritual presence in the Universe, but that there is a greater presence —God or absolute reality—and that the true end of Man is to place himself in harmony with this.

It might be argued that, even with the near-universality of the religious impulse admitted, this does not necessarily range human nature in opposition to Communism, if Communism can satify the religious impulse. But here we are perilously close to playing with words. Communism may attempt to usurp the place of religion, in the kind of devotion it tries to exact, in the dogmas it propounds for creating a good life on earth, in the heaven on earth promised by the Marxian Utopia, and in the rigorous discipline and subordination of propagators of the Communist doctrine. But none of this is relevant to the true inner religious feeling of man, a feeling which reaches out beyond the material world and strives for spiritual understanding.

Communism may supply the trappings of religious fanaticism, but it cannot supply any of the inner substance of religion. It cannot help the Russian parent when his child asks, "Who made the world?"

The religious impulse is a striving to find God. It will not be satisfied with worshiping a theoretical earthly Utopia, an intangible political philosophy, or even a tangible brand-new tractor.

Chapter FIVE

The Future of What We Are For

We began with these propositions: What we are for is the active force for constructive change in the world; most people in the world want change; and the purpose of stating what we are for is to achieve "identification," by showing others that it will help advance their plans to change their lives and societies for the better.

How well is this process of identification succeeding, and how well is it likely to succeed?

To answer this question clearly, we must look at the countries of the world in three groups: the mature economies of the free world; the newly-developing countries of the free world; and the countries of the Communist bloc. These represent an ascending order of difficulty, so far as the task of identification is concerned. They are, so to speak, the positive, comparative, and superlative of the problem.

The Mature Economies of the Free World

If we can detach ourselves from the everyday scenes of turmoil, tension, rock-throwing, and embassy-smashing, and acquire a historical perspective, we will descry an unmistakable fact: *The world in recent years has definitely been moving in the direction of what we are for.*

Once in a great while history turns a corner. The people living through the event are seldom aware of it, but over a span of twenty or thirty years the change of direction becomes visible.

Such a turn occurred in the years after World War II. For decades, and certainly during the thirties and forties, it was widely assumed that the entire world was moving in the direction of statism and nationalization of industry. Even in Britain it seemed to be taken for granted that the process of nationalizing industries would go steadily forward, industry by industry. As for the United States, most intellectuals, whether they liked the idea or not, proceeded on the premise that the world's direction was being set by Europe, and that it was only a matter of time—ten or twenty years—before the United States would follow in the footsteps of Britain.

Then, in recent years, a number of things happened to bend the course of events. The United States took a firm line whose direction was drawn from American traditions of federal-state balance of power, executive-legislative division of function, respect for private enterprise, and a presumption in favor of the private way of doing things. At the same time, the United States demonstrated that the best elements of this tradition could be effectively combined with the best elements of social, welfare, and regulatory legislation.

People began to discover that other countries were pursuing a similar course. West Germany put into effect a lusty enterprise democracy program. Private enterprise began producing obvious results in such places as Italy and Japan. Gradually a general truth began to be evident: *The degree to which a country made postwar economic strides was closely related to the degree to which it pursued enterprise democracy methods.* Britain, looking about her at some of these other countries, had sober second thoughts about nationalizing industries. The experience with those that had been nationalized proved that nationalization solves practically none of the problems it is

122

supposed to solve, not even labor relations, and causes new problems to arise. Britain stopped the nationalizing trend dead in its tracks, and indeed reversed it by proceeding to "denationalize" such businesses as road transport and steel.

The state of public opinion in all industrialized countries outside the Communist bloc turned overwhelmingly against nationalization.

A public opinion poll was taken by the international polling expert, Elmo C. Wilson, and published in his bulletin of February, 1958, on this question:

Which of these policies toward big industries do you think the government of this country should follow: leave them strictly alone under their own management and ownership; regulate them enough to see that they don't take advantage of the public but don't try to manage them; take over the ownership and management of large industries?

For our purposes, the first two options can be added together, since they are on the enterprise democracy side, and the "don't know" responses, which were in most cases quite small, can be left out for the sake of simplicity. Here are the results:

	Leave Them Alone or Regulate but Don't Manage	Take Them Over
SWEDEN	81%	5%
AUSTRALIA	88%	6%
BRITAIN	84%	8%
NORWAY	73%	3%
NETHERLANDS	83%	5%
AUSTRIA	77%	13%
BRAZIL	61%	10%
BELGIUM	66%	7%
DENMARK	73%	4%
FRANCE	72%	14%
ITALY	63%	19%
GERMANY	77%	4%
CANADA	81%	5%
JAPAN	45%	18%

The real significance of this crushingly one-sided demonstration of world opinion seems to be this: Demand for heavy and detailed governmental involvement in the economy, including government ownership, is now seen to be a transitional and passing phase, or at best a partial solution of particular problems. It is necessary to some extent in newly developing countries which cannot muster private capital and industry fast enough in any other way. But in an established industrial economy it is out of place and does not work.

Even socialist parties are beginning to accept this truth as a matter of official policy when they are located in industrialized countries.

For example, we read the following in an Associated Press dispatch of April 30, 1958:

A policy commission of the West German Socialist Party today abandoned the traditional demand for state ownership of all major industries and called for a state-guided free economy.

Public ownership was recommended for only two industries—coal and nuclear energy.

Similarly, in July, 1958, a working group of the British Labour Party's national executive published a "plan for progress" which relies not on nationalization but on expansionism and high investment in a capitalist economy guided by the state.

As for the Communist Party in the industrialized countries, it is rapidly being seen to have lost its reason for existence. It survives as a vehicle for general protest, but only a small minority of the people really adhere to

125

its principles or program. This was plainly evident in France during the 1958 crisis. Although 5 million votes had been cast for Communist candidates in the 1956 elections, the Communist Party was completely unable to deliver on the "action" and "strikes" it threatened. It has been estimated that the number of actual members of the Communist Party in France is less than 600,000, and that the number who could be relied on for real action in a crisis is perhaps a tenth of that.

Whatever were the reasons for the movement toward nationalization of industry in mature countries, it is now clear that the movement has not proved itself and is emphatically rejected by the people of all those countries.

The underlying facts, then, on which mutual understanding on political-economic principles can rest are more favorable now in these countries than they have been for many years.

The Newly Developing Countries

The task of achieving identification with the newly developing countries is markedly different.

The nub of the problem here can be concisely put. The set of facts to which political-economic ideas must be related in a country like India is sharply different from the set of facts to which these ideas are related in the United States and the maturer economies. India's task is to create a modern agriculture and industry. The task of the maturer countries is to bring an existing highly developed economy and government to maximum efficiency and equity in serving the needs of their people.

How then can we achieve identification?

The mistake of supposing that the details and mechanisms of an American type of private enterprise system can be superimposed upon the Indian scene has already been quite thoroughly exposed. But in its place is appearing another mistake at the opposite extreme: the mistake of supposing that the task India and similar countries face is so different from ours that there is no carry-over of principle at all.

The correct view is that there are certain deep-seated principles that are just as valid in India as they are in the United States. Granted a similar objective—the raising of living standards of human beings through industrialization and modern techniques—any country, whatever its present condition, must respect these ultimate principles if it is to reach that objective. This can be proved as a matter of both common sense and demonstrated experience. Among these principles are those that have been discussed in this book: the Lincoln formula on the role of government; the necessity for having not just one entity but at least three entities—business, labor, and government—actively working toward the objective; the

127

acceptance of the mutual interest of those three entities; the determining of all questions on a broad, long-range basis in terms of time, space, and interest; and the aligning of governmental and economic arrangements with the basic drives and motivations of human nature.

In negative terms: A dictated, state-owned economy never has created or administered in any country, and never can create or administer in any country, a modern industrial economy geared to raising the standard of living of people.

We are here concerned, not with the capacity to build up, regardless of purpose, a big industrial machine. We are concerned with the ability to construct an economy which, by use of industrialization and other modern techniques, *rapidly raises the living standards of people.*

Of all the fundamentals at stake here, none is more basic than the relation of government to the economy and to people. We may use this relation then, to show how the essence of enterprise domocracy has universal validity, although the details of its application may vary.

The essence of what we are for, on this point, is summed up in the Lincoln formula, discussed at the beginning of the second chapter: The function of government is to do for people what needs to be done, but what they cannot do at all for themselves, or do so well. This is the underlying common denominator we can use to identify ourselves with the efforts of newly developing countries everywhere.

When you transplant this formula to India, for example, you find that there is much more that needs to be done for the people, and that there is a much larger part of it that they cannot do for themselves through private means. But the principle itself is just as valid, although the facts are changed.

It may be that a chemical fertilizer plant is needed. And it may be that there is no private organization that has the capital to build a chemical fertilizer plant. If, then, the government initiates the construction of the plant, it is quite possible that this is consistent with the Lincoln formula, just as if the United States built a synthetic-rubber plant in time of emergency, which it has been known to do.

What, then, is the difference between this view and the acceptance of nationalization of industry as a general principle?

The difference is crucial. It is between government ownership or involvement as a transitional or limited device, and as a permanent feature of a developed economy.

Government stimulation, financing, and even ownership of means of production can be justified as a way of getting an economy started in a newly developing country. But the same nationalization that might be a needed device to get things started in a new economy is, as we have seen, a deadening drag upon a developed economy, and is now overwhelmingly rejected by the people of every major free-world country.

Under the Lincoln formula, when the governmental stimulus or initiative has served its purpose, and when adequate private capital and management have been developed, the government should normally try to turn over to private enterprise those businesses that can best be operated privately.

A good case study of this formula in action is the Commonwealth of Puerto Rico. The Puerto Rican government, under the leadership of Governor Muñoz Marin, has vigorously taken the initiative in getting all kinds of industries and commercial ventures started. But no one calls the Puerto Rican development program statism. The reason is clear. Governor Muñoz adheres scrupulously to his policy of getting the government out of businesses when the govermental participation has done its work. The ultimate goal is always an economy as private as circumstances allow.

The importance of the distinction between enterprise democracy as an ultimate goal and a state-owned economy as an ultimate goal may not seem important in the early stages of a country's economic development, when it is a long way from either. But the only reliable way to judge your principles and your direction is to extrapolate the line you are following and see what kind of system you will have at the end.

That system must be able to answer efficiently the great economic questions of who makes what, who gets what, and how much, in such a way as to produce maximum prosperity and equity. Soviet Communism destroys the natural mechanisms for providing an answer: free-market prices, competition, profits, free labor organization, wage bargaining, business failure and success. What can it put in their place?

In the last analysis, although Communism or any other possible completely nationalized economy can of course make some use of artificially fixed prices, incentives, and other borrowed private enterprise features, there is only one purely statist regulator available to the completely state-planned, state-administered economy: the compulsory quota. Since there is no free, competitive price system or profit system to tell businessmen what to make or sell, they must be told from above by the planners, through the device of the imposed quota.

The relative efficacy of free enterprise principles and

totalitarian principles in creating and running a modern industrial economy can therefore in large measure be boiled down to a comparison of the efficacy of natural free-market regulators and of the compulsory quota.

This comparison, both in theory and in observed practice in Communist countries, demonstrates that at every point the natural regulators contain a built-in stimulant favoring high standards of production for consumers, and the quota system contains a built-in bias toward failure of production for consumers. Let us look at several examples.

1. Free enterprise has a *built-in stimulant to high production*. Ordinarily, high production means efficiency, reduced relative overhead costs, and progressively increasing profits. It is limited only by consumer demand, and in modern times this demand has risen by the complementary process of the growth of high wages well distributed among workers.

The quota system contains a *built-in bias toward low production*. Put yourself in the place of a Soviet plant manager. Since your fortunes depend on overfulfilling your quotas, your strongest motive is to get your quota set as *low* as possible in the first place. You marshal every argument, you pull every string, you influence every official you can—to get your production sights set low.

132

If productivity is the aim, the system is hardly off to a flying start.

Now, someone might say that, having got a low quota, you will then overfulfill to the utmost. But not so fast! There is next year to consider. If you overfulfill by too much, your reward will be to get saddled with a still higher quota for the following year. The next thing you know, you will have a quota you cannot meet. You have not forgotten those managers who went to jail as counter-revolutionaries for this kind of crime. And so you produce just enough to make a good showing, but not so much as to cause you a problem for the future.

2. The enterprise system has a *built-in stimulant to efficiency*. The more carefully a manager analyzes and reduces his costs, the more conscientiously he maintains and repairs his machinery, the more prudently he uses his materials and resources, the more profits he will make. Conversely, if he is lax in these respects, the relentless laws of competitive survival will weed him out and leave the field to the efficient.

The quota system has a *built-in bias against efficiency*. Suppose you are a mine manager trying to meet a tough quota. Since you will be judged only by your quantitative production record, you race through the easy-to-mine areas, leaving harder-to-mine ore untouched. You neglect normal mining practices that would leave the mine in good shape as you go along. This kind of inefficiency, which has characterized Soviet mining, would bankrupt a private enterprise mine.

Similarly, there is nothing in the quota system to encourage the repair and maintenance practices that a modern factory must have, since the time and resources spent on repair merely cut into the quota.

The enterprise system has a *built-in stimulant to innovation*. Consumers are always quick to reward the manufacturer who has a new or better product, or the shop that has a new or better service. Patent laws ensure handsome prizes to the ingenious and resourceful, and to the first manufacturer in the field with an improved machine or appliance or invention.

The quota system has a *built-in bias against innovation*. The Soviet plant manager is loath to reduce his quantitative output in order to divert men and materials to the design and production of an unfamiliar item. Thus, Mr. Pavlov, Soviet Minister of Trade, complains in a 1958 *Izvestia* article that new products such as potato-peeling machines were not coming on the market, although scheduled for two years earlier.

4. The enterprise system has a *built-in stimulant to quality*. The consumer will choose the better-quality item

in a competitive situation, and obviously the manufacturer and seller who offer the higher quality will have the better business and reap the greater profits. Those who offer defective or second-rate goods will be driven to the wall.

The quota system has a *built-in bias against quality*. After all, if your quota is ten thousand radios, you will meet it just as well with five thousand somewhat defective but passable radios and five thousand moderately shoddy radios as with ten thousand superbly crafted and finished radios. This accounts for the frequent rumblings we hear from within the Soviet Union, both from the government and from consumers, about bad workmanship and sleazy quality.

5. The enterprise system has a *built-in stimulant to good consumer service*. Merely supplying a product is not enough to survive in competition. Courteous attention, good repair and parts facilities, commercial responsibility —all these are important to the consumer and essential to the prosperity of the businessman.

The quota system has a *built-in bias against good consumer service*. The obvious reason is that such service does not count on the quota. You may wonder why, when the Soviet manufacturers in their haste to make their quotas flood the stores with defective merchandise, the stores themselves do not reject the goods. The reason is that the stores themselves have sales quotas to meet! And why should anyone make spare parts? They do not count in the quota either.

6. The enterprise system has a *built-in stimulant to the efficient distribution* of materials and products. The price mechanism automatically draws them to the point where they are most needed, from the point where they are in best supply.

The quota system has a *built-in bias against efficient distribution* of materials and products. Suppose Plant A has managed to hoard a ten-year supply of titanium, and Plant B in the same town is shut down for lack of titanium. Will the titanium move from Plant A to Plant B? Why should it? There is nothing in the Communist system to encourage it legally to make the move. Indeed, the manager of Plant A will jealously hide the fact of his titanium surplus and cling to his supply with all his might, because some day he might himself need titanium he cannot get.

Examples of this kind could be multiplied, and in every case backed up with reports of actual events that have taken place within the Communist countries, in many instances drawn from their own official sources.

The Communist authorities try to meet these inherent

deficiencies by injecting private enterprise features, principally an elaborate incentive system that can only be described as an artificial statist attempt to duplicate the profit system. To the extent that they do this, they achieve some success. But the frantic attempts of planners to anticipate and approximate the myriad great and small adjustments of a modern economy can never begin to take the place of the natural and automatic adjustments that a free economy makes.

The modern economy is not a machine; it is a living organism of incredible complexity. Suppose that a planner decided that he was going to anticipate and plan all the adjustments that a human body makes in the course of a day. He might manage to think of the most important— to have the body temperature mechanisms adjust when the weather gets hotter, to turn on a certain amount of perspiration, to signal for more drinking water, to turn on this gland and turn off that gland. But will he remember to be sure to make the eyelid blink each time a small foreign object flies toward it? Can he tell the organism just when to change its metabolism rate and alter its pulse beat and raise up goose-pimples and blow its nose?

A human organism dependent on this kind of planning would not survive until lunch time.

The feverish efforts of the Soviet Union's central planners to apply stimulants, and then checks upon the stimulants, and then correctives upon the checks, are becoming a familiar story. For example, in order to stimulate meat production, farmers were allowed to raise cattle and pigs on their private plots and sell the meat in a free market. At the same time, bread was being sold at an artificially low price on the controlled market. The farmers discovered that they could buy up the bread at the low fixed prices, feed it to their cattle and pigs, and turn a nice profit in the process. Entire enterprises for converting bread to beef and pork sprang up. Trucks made the rounds of bakeries, cleaning them out of bread. The result, then, of a measure designed to increase the food supply was to create a shortage of bread for human consumption! The corrective was more controls, bread rationing, criminal punishment for feeding bread to stock, and severe taxing of stock-raising in cities.

And so it goes. The harassed planner, armed with a whole dispensary full of assorted hypodermic injections, strait jackets, splints, sedatives, and no-doze pills, tries with diminishing success to duplicate the stimulants and regulators which, left to their own normal functioning, would do the job effortlessly and automatically.

Do we have to put people in jail to cure them of feeding pigs on sandwiches? No, because a free market for both bread and meat makes this as uneconomic as it sounds ridiculous.

The principal point of this review of the contrast between how enterprise principles naturally favor effective consumer production and how totalitarian principles naturally disfavor it, is not to belittle the Soviet accomplishments. It is rather to make the affirmative point of interest to the newly developing countries: that there is a certain amount of basic principle that has validity in all countries. A country which wishes to provide a good life for its people in the era of industrialization can align itself with the natural forces of human nature and economic law which will create that good life, or it can try to overrule and outguess these forces. Both courses have been tried. The results are open for all to see.

Someone at this point is certainly bursting to ask this question: If Communism is so ill-adapted to a modern industrial economy, how do you account for the tremendous strides made in the industrialization of Russia?

One answer is this: the Soviets have demonstrated their ability to create a huge war-directed and war-supporting industry and technology; they have failed utterly to create an economy that takes care of the wants and needs of consumers. This is an entirely different problem, and one that is a hundred times more difficult.

139

Since the first earth satellite was launched, a large part of the world has been taken in by one of the most colossal *non sequiturs* in history: the assumption that, because the Soviets could build up highly-advanced weapons and huge war-supporting heavy industry, the Communist system held the key to fast industrialization and accelerated production for a consumer-based economy.

Exactly what have the Soviet successes proved?

They have proved something we already knew, which is that a dictatorship can concentrate the resources of a large country and produce truly spectacular results—in a relatively narrow area.

We saw Hitler do it. We saw Mussolini do it. We could trace the pattern all the way back to the Pharaohs, who built some very impressive pyramids and filled them with thousands of magnificent figurines, jewels, and golden ornaments.

The Pharaohs built pyramids. The Soviet dictators built a gigantic technically-advanced war machine, together with the heavy industry, specialized educational facilities, and scientific establishment needed to support it.

The Soviets, having impressed the world with genuinely remarkable scientific feats in the realm of missiles and the like, parade before the world statistics on steel production, coal production, power production, and other heavy-industry advances—and then take a flying leap to the conclusion that this all equals increased well-being for people, if not actual, at least potential and just around the corner. In actual fact, it equals nothing of the sort.

Before going further, we should take a moment to set the record straight on the extent to which the Soviet accomplishment suggests the solution to the problems which confront the countries of Asia, Africa, and Latin America.

It has become almost habitual nowadays to say that the Soviet Union has transformed a backward agrarian land into a highly developed industrial economy in forty years.

We are supposed to infer from this that a miracle of speedy progress has been accomplished which has no earthly parallel.

We can give credit where credit is due without going overboard into romantic distortions of history like this one. The story needs trimming at both ends.

To begin with, the Soviet Union did not begin with as benighted and blighted and backward a country as this account assumes. It began with the sixth largest economy in the world. Its per capita production was even then much larger than that of today's newly developing countries. Its educational standards under the Czars were as high as those of such continental countries as Germany and Switzerland.

Here, then, was an enormous country, with a giant productive potential, getting a somewhat belated start in the Industrial Revolution. It was greatly aided by tremendous injections of foreign capital and foreign technical assistance, by lend-lease equipment during the War, and by machinery and capital goods carried off after the War.

Even so, the Soviets' rate of progress has been no greater than that of other countries in comparable periods. Canada, for example, was growing even faster during exactly the same period, and in a much better proportioned and sounder way. Since World War II, a number of other countries, such as Western Germany, have had rates of growth much greater than the Soviets'.

Just as the Soviets did not start from as far back as they claim, so they have not come anywhere near as far forward as they would like to have us believe. We are talking now of living standards, not gross tonnages or millions of kilowatt hours.

The absolute statistics from official Soviet sources themselves show that, as far as the two great essentials of food and shelter are concerned, the people of the Soviet

Union as a whole are little better off than they were under the last Czar.

The official United Nations study confirms that Russian housing standards are the lowest in Europe.

Of course, there are some improvements. Clothing is better. Some consumer goods begin to make their appearance from time to time.

But the main argument is not going to stand or fall on variations in the interpretation of statistics on milk or shoe production. The main argument is this: Granted that the Soviet Union has the resources, the manpower, the scientific acumen, and the industrial potential to give her people a good standard of living; a Communist regime, *applying Communist ideas,* can not do so, and has not done so, and will not do so.

It is a temptation to jump to the conclusion that, having mastered the problem of technology and production for a war machine, the Soviets can now at will turn a different spigot and proceed to draw off great quantities of consumer goods which will be distributed lavishly to the happy Russian workers.

The indisputable historic fact is this: *No dictator has ever solved the economic problem of production and distribution for use and enjoyment by consumers.*

There have been plenty of absolutist regimes that had

at their disposal the economic wherewithal to spread around a good standard of living—but they never did.

The Pharaohs *could* have taken their marvelous pyramid construction industry and converted it into the building of model housing developments for workers—but they never did.

Hitler *could* have delivered those 330,000 Volkswagens that the German people bought and paid for—but he never did. He built armaments instead. It remained for the postwar democracy to build and deliver the Volkswagens.

The Soviet Union *could* have devoted at least some reasonable proportion of its gross national product to raising living standards, as every other civilized country has done—but it never has. Three times as much of its national product, in proportion to ours, goes into the war machine and war-supporting industry.

This is no mere coincidence. Behind this fact lies the stark fact that the economic problem of production and distribution for consumer use is entirely different from that of production for expansion and war.

The two great parts of the economic problem are production and distribution.

As to production: An authoritarian regime need not worry about demand or what to produce. Demand is infinite. You can always build more armaments, just as you can always build more pyramids. Because demand is unlimited, such a regime can boast that it has no business cycles, no question of adequate investment, no unemployment.

As to distribution: It is dictated by a simple formula, which is to spread goods around as incentives in such a way as to forward the overriding goals of increased arms development, the support of scientific progress, cultural and propaganda measures, and other expansionist aims.

Now, how do you move from an economy constructed around these principles to one based on consumer needs and desires—and still retain your totalitarian principles and objectives?

Of course, the Soviet authorities will from time to time allow a greater supply of consumer goods to be made and distributed. This does not alter the central fact that the sovereign test of both production and distribution is still what serves the ends of the state and the rulers. The reasons, within that framework, that might lead to more consumer goods include: to increase incentive in the right places, since eventually more money without more goods to spend it on ceases to be an incentive; for propaganda reasons, to remove the disgrace of poverty which is becoming increasingly known abroad; to forestall anti-regime resentment; and to make good in part on the big promises of Khrushchev.

The possibility of this kind of limited increase in consumer goods is not the point. The point is that *an economy directed by the state will ultimately always serve the ends of the state. Only an economy directed by consumers will ultimately serve the needs of consumers.*

So far, the advantages to the newly developing countries of enterprise democracy over a state-owned economy have been presented as if nothing counted but the relative ability of the systems to produce material well-being for people. The object was to demonstrate that, on this testing-ground alone, enterprise democracy has the overwhelming advantage.

But enterprise democracy provides all this, and along with it the immeasurable treasure of freedom. To most people in the world, eager as they are for material progress, a system which offered material well-being only at the price of personal freedom would be out of the question. Yet totalitarian Communism not only defaults on the job of creating a prosperous modern consumer economy, but for this dismal performance still exacts the price of personal freedom.

The reason this must inevitably happen in a state with

146

full government ownership of the economy has already been discussed in Chapter 2, under the heading, "The Presumption in Favor of the Non-Governmental." The deadly combination of full economic and full political-military power in the government's hands cannot possibly leave any basis on which the individual could enforce personal rights or freedoms in a showdown.

It does not detract from this statement to point to personal freedoms in some free-world countries that have sometimes loosely been called "socialist." The term "socialism" has been studiously avoided in this book, since it has come to mean anything from complete government ownership and operation of all means of production to an undefined amount of government regulation and social welfare activity. The most that has occurred in the way of "socialism" outside the Communist bloc has been an attempt to superimpose upon an essentially private-property economy some fragments of nationalized industry or communications or services. The amount of economic power remaining in nongovernment hands is still relatively very large and decisively preponderant. Accordingly, the kind of absolute power which results in absolute tyranny does not appear.

Therefore, those "socialists" in newly developing countries whose public sector amounts to perhaps ten per cent, and who see no threats to personal freedom from this ten per cent, must be careful not to make the tragic error of supposing that freedom could survive a public sector of ninety per cent. The difference is that, in the former case, the essential tone and balance of power in the society is being set by its private character. In the latter case, the nature of society will be dictated by the relentless formula: $T = E + P$. Tyranny equals economic power plus political power in the same hands.

It remains a provable historical fact that full-blown state ownership of the economy has never existed side by side with personal freedom. Enterprise democracy and totalitarian Communism are consistent with themselves. You can no more have enterprise democracy without freedom than you can have totalitarian Communism with freedom. It takes freedom to make the former function. It takes dictation to make the latter function.

In summary: The newly developing countries, and specifically the active, educated groups most eager to forward their countries' rapid development, will find in enterprise democracy the two things they most want: swift improvement in living conditions through industrialization and modern techniques, and the self-fulfillment that goes with personal and national freedom. This being so, the bond of identification that we feel with these countries and these groups should—and will, when the true facts are understood—be full and generous and confident.

The People within the Communist Bloc

It was said at the beginning of the chapter that the world is moving toward what we are for.

The most remarkable, dramatic, and paradoxical proof of this statement is the direction of events within the Soviet bloc itself.

The Soviets have scored notable successes in certain lines of effort, and they should be given credit for these achievements. But we are here concerned not with the relative effectiveness of peoples or countries but with the relative effectiveness of *ideas*.

One can therefore make full acknowledgment of the accomplishments of the Soviet Union as a country and a people, and still say this:

The areas in which the Soviets have had their greatest successes are the very areas in which they have to the greatest degree abandoned their own principles and copied ours.

As the truth of this statement more and more permeates the thought of high Soviet officials, the process of scrapping Communist dogma and adopting enterprise principles gains momentum.

149

The most fundamental example of this is the objective of the system itself. The enterprise system has always stressed the objective of *high productivity*. Americans take this for granted. But to appreciate the shift of emphasis this involves for Communism, one must recall that during much of the last hundred years, two ideas have been competing on how best to raise the lot of the workingman.

The one idea is central to private enterprise thought. It stresses production. It holds that if everyone concentrates on increasing production, there will be much more for all to share, and the standard of living of the worker will thus be raised more effectively than in any other way.

The other idea is central to Marxian thought. It stresses distribution. It holds that the best way to improve the position of the worker is to expropriate the owners' properties and redistribute them on a basis more favorable to workers.

The contrast between leveling distribution and increasing production was never better stated than in the famous saying of Abraham Lincoln:

Let not him who is houseless pull down the house of another, but let him work diligently and build one for himself.

The orthodox Communist approach, stressing redistribution instead of production, is illustrated by Stalin's handling of the problem of food supply. Stalin seemed to have the obsession that the solution to the food supply problem was to extort a larger proportion of food out of the grasp of the farmers.

But at the same time the five-year plans gradually were promoting productivity as a goal in itself. Now Khrushchev has completely abandoned the Marxian approach, has found quotations from Lenin to support his position, and has wholeheartedly embraced the enterprise democracy idea of raising everyone's share by increasing the total supply. To the extent he succeeds—and no one can hope for anything but success in a venture to put more food in the mouths of people—this will be one more testimonial, not to the productivity of Communist ideas, but to the efficacy of private enterprise ideas and aims.

If Marx were to visit Russia today, he would receive nothing but a series of severe shocks to discover that the flat contrary of all the things he preached was being done in his name. Indeed, even before his death he had made the poignant statement, "I am not a Marxist." But of all the shocks, none would be more astonishing than the discovery that the case for the superiority of Communism over capitalism was being heavily based on the claim that capitalism was unable to compete in the field of productivity.

Economic writers have produced, surprisingly, many passages of rich, beautiful prose. But none of them can touch the lyrical praise lavished by Marx, in the opening pages of the *Communist Manifesto,* on the inherent productive power of bourgeois capitalism. Listen to these excerpts:

The bourgeoisie, during its rule of scarce one hundred years, has created more massive and more colossal productive forces than have all preceding generations together.

Subjection of Nature's forces to man, machinery, application of chemistry to industry and agriculture, steam navigation, railways, electric telegraphs, clearing of whole continents for cultivation, canalization of rivers, whole populations conjured out of the ground . . .

It has accomplished wonders far surpassing Egyptian pyramids, Roman aqueducts, and Gothic cathedrals; it has conducted expeditions that put in the shade all former Exoduses of nations and crusades.

Indeed, no one can pretend to understand the central theme of Marx's own doctrine unless he clearly comprehends that Marx's criticism of capitalism was not that it was insufficiently productive but that it was far too productive! This restless overproductiveness, in turn, was the

152

cause of the injustices and crises that would eventually
destroy capitalism, in Marx's view. But let him speak for
himself:

The bourgeoisie cannot exist without constantly revolu-
tionizing the instruments of production. . . . All old-estab-
lished national industries have been destroyed or are daily
being destroyed. They are dislodged by new industries, whose
introduction becomes a life and death question for all civilized nations, by industries that no longer work up indigenous
raw material, but raw material drawn from the remotest
zones; industries whose products are consumed, not only at
home, but in every quarter of the globe. . . . And as in
material, so also in intellectual production.

So far, in modern ears, this sounds pretty good. But
now comes the dénouément:

Modern bourgeois society with its relations of production,
of exchange and of property, a society that has conjured up
such gigantic means of production and of exchange, is like
a sorcerer, who is no longer able to control the powers of
the nether world whom he has called up by his spells. . . . In
these crises there breaks out an epidemic that, in all earlier
epochs, would have seemed an absurdity—the epidemic of
overproduction . . . and why? Because there is too much
civilization, *too much means of subsistence, too much industry, too much commerce.*   [Italics supplied.]

153

It may be safely assumed that, when Communists preach to Asians, Africans, and Latin Americans about what system will best increase their means of subsistence and industry, they do not use this passage as their text. The "evil" of too much industry, too much means of subsistence, and too much commerce is one with which most Asian, African, and Latin American countries would undoubtedly be glad to take their chances.

A second illustration of the Communists' producing results by jettisoning their doctrines and emulating ours is their repeated use of *the incentive principle* whenever production must be stimulated.

This has always been one of the mainsprings of private enterprise. Prizes for energy and ingenuity, punishments for laziness and stupidity—these are built into the very structure of our system.

Orthodox Communism, on the other hand, affected to look down on the acquisitive and competitive instincts.

The Communists discovered almost at once, however, that human nature was human nature even after a Communist revolution, and they proceeded to superimpose incentives artificially upon their system. Now they have carried them in many instances far beyond anything in our own country. For example, as Djilas points out in *The New Class,* the secretary of the Rayon Committee in the U. S. S. R. gets twenty-five times the compensation of an ordinary worker. In the United States, even a Cabinet member is paid only about five or six times as much as the average industrial worker.

Since, in the Soviet Union, the state controls all wages and controls the availability of almost all goods and services, it is plainly in a position to use this power to apply incentives in such a way as to forward state policies and objectives. This is precisely what it does. Sometimes the connection is not evident on the surface, until you remember how the Soviets press into the service of their expansionist drive a wide variety of sectors of their resources and culture.

It is easy to understand why a bureaucrat or a scientist is paid many times what a worker gets, in view of Soviet objectives. Or to understand why a science professor may get the equivalent of $30,000 or $40,000 a year, although some other teachers are underpaid. In the same way, other intellectuals, professors, performing artists, and technicians may be highly paid if their activities are relevant to the furtherance of Soviet industrial, military, propaganda, or economic purposes.

Where this relevance is not thought to exist, the high incentive pay does not exist either—even for scientific and intellectual activity.

A stunning example is the low pay of doctors. In the United States, doctors are the highest paid of all professional people. It could well be argued that this is a reflection of the high value placed on the individual human being's life and health.

But in the U. S. S. R., it is quite common to find in an industrial plant that the physicians are being paid about one-half the wage of a good industrial worker. Except for certain specialists with advanced degrees, and medical administrators, the doctors are the lowest-paid professional people in the U. S. S. R.

The practice of relying on property incentives and the efficacy of this private enterprise motivation have become so thoroughly accepted in Soviet thought that Soviet leaders now almost automatically turn to these methods when the need for increased production is urgent.

Almost since the beginning of the Soviet story, whenever a situation developed that called for a sharp increase in production we heard the following line of ideological rationalization emanating from within the Soviet Union: It is all right temporarily to allow private production or a free market, so as to get the necessary production to tide over the emergency; but, after this temporary deviation in the interests of productivity, we will then resume the orthodox road to Communism.

Now, the question that leaps out at you from this rationale is a blunt one: If Communism is more productive than private enterprise, why, when the need is for more production, do you not apply more Communism, rather than less?

The earliest instance of this deliberate abandonment of Communism in the interests of productivity was the N. E. P. in the early twenties.

In 1921 there was a severe drought in the Soviet Union and the need for action to increase the supply of food was acute. Under the N. E. P., farmers were for a few years allowed to engage in private farming. The result was a terrific upsurge of production.

In recent years, with production the watchword, Mr. Khrushchev has repeatedly and increasingly applied comparable incentive techniques to agriculture. For example, farmers were allowed to sell the produce of their tiny private plots, and meat from privately-owned livestock, on a free market. The prices were set by competition and by demand, in the best private enterprise tradition. The result: In four years the number of beef cattle multiplied four times over, while the number of beef cattle on collectives virtually did not increase at all. Half the hog and cow increases, and two-thirds of the sheep and goat increases between 1953 and 1958 were in the private sector.

157

In 1958, a far-reaching revision of Soviet agriculture in the direction of enterprise and incentive was undertaken. Instead of forced deliveries and complicated formulas for payment, the new system abolished compulsory deliveries to the state and set uniform prices for a given grade of product in a given area. Profits under the new system will thus depend on efficiency, just as in a private enterprise system. A parallel move, combining incentive, decentralization, and the principle of property, was the decision to allow the collective farms to buy up the tractors and farm machinery formerly controlled by the state tractor stations.

This last move occurred not long after Mr. Vladimir V. Matskevich, Agriculture Minister, and his colleagues visited Iowa. They saw how a typical Iowa farmer could keep his tractor busy a large part of the time, because it was always where he wanted it when he needed it. He had fifteen or twenty ingenious tractor appliances, and could make use of the tractor almost every day.

And so, once more, Communist political orthodoxy gave way to the demands of productivity. The collectives were permitted gradually to buy their own tractors, and make their own decisions on how and when and where to use them.

A similar story is being repeated in other Communist

countries. Poland in 1956 sharply decreased the proportion of state and collective farming and put agriculture largely on a private enterprise basis. By 1958, collective farms were down to 2 per cent of Polish agriculture. The result: Almost overnight grains became so abundant that it was difficult to find a place to put the surplus grain sent from America, and there was actually a surplus of milk.

Mr. Khrushchev is a realist first and an ideologist second. He knows that Soviet food production must be substantially increased. He knows that the farmers of the United States, comprising only one-eighth of our population, not only provide our own people with a high-quality diet but supply food to many other parts of the world, and at the same time amass awkward surpluses, in spite of elaborate government schemes to hold down production. He knows that *half* of the Soviet population works on farms and can scarcely supply the Soviet people with more than a subsistence diet.

There must be a reason. And when you add together these facts, plus the N. E. P. experience, plus the experience of the private plots and stock in the U. S. S. R. since 1953, plus the experience of Poland and other Communist countries, the elementary human-nature reason is plain to any realist: The more scope you give to incentive and freedom, the more production you get.

159

In industry, as in agriculture, resort to private-property incentives to elicit production has become commonplace in the Soviet Union.

For example, in the case of Mr. Pavlov and his elusive potato-peelers mentioned earlier, here was his proposed solution, as reported by the Associated Press on February 26, 1958:

He suggested production could be stimulated by increasing the wholesale price 3.5 per cent and rewarding factory officials and workers who turn out more peelers.

In the industrial area, as in the farm area, a parallel trend can be observed in other Communist countries. For example, here is a resolution of the Central Committee of the Czechoslovak Communist Party made on February 25, 1958, as reported by Reuters:

The resolution said the present system of organizing and directing the economy "no longer corresponds today to the needs of a rapidly expanding economy". . .

Factories will be allowed to share in the profit from their own production so as to give them a financial basis to decide independently about their own investment, general repairs, and other projects.

Thus it happens that when one begins to use the language of "rapidly expanding economy," one also quite naturally begins to use the language of independent investment and profit.

A third illustration of how Soviet success is related to emulation of our principles is *the principle of freedom of thought*.

Freedom of thought has always been at the very heart of our tradition.

Uncompromising intolerance of freedom of thought has been the hallmark of the Communist movement for a century.

Except for a very brief period immediately after the Revolution, ruthless repression of any originality of thought has been the standard order of procedure in the U. S. S. R. It was an article of faith with men like Stalin that if the germ of freedom of thought were allowed to appear in painting, or musical composition, or poetry, or novels, or architecture, or any other department of art or creativity, the entire Soviet power mechanism would be in danger.

But in one area, this enmity to freedom of thought collided head-on with another Soviet compulsion of even higher priority: the need for technological and scientific progress to strengthen the country's military power. Lenin had plainly taught that Communism must learn to press into service every kind of weapon of modern war, including the most advanced. In the scientific age, this meant that huge old-fashioned land armies were not enough. It followed that the Soviets must make rapid advances in science.

But this ambition encountered the stark fact that scientific discovery cannot be dictated, and that test tubes are no respecters of commissars. Stalin could perhaps, without damaging the arms program, play at omniscience in the field of genetics by dictating the validity of Lysenko's theory and sending to Siberia any biologist who disagreed. But he could not dictate that rocket fuel A is in harmony with the Party Line and that rocket fuel B is not—that is, not if he wanted to get a rocket off the ground.

Even Stalin would eventually have to concede that the scientists must be free to think, imagine, experiment, disagree, and draw conclusions—within their precise realm of physical science related to war, expansion, or propaganda aims.

This kind of concession did not come easily, suddenly, or completely to Josef Stalin. (And it still has not come to Communist China—which seems determined to repeat most of the Soviet Union's mistakes, at a respectful distance in time.) There was a considerable period during which Stalin seemed to be bothered by the question whether quantum mechanics was good Marxism. This theory, which lies at the very foundation of today's physics, apparently caused quite an argument among Communist ideologists. Of course, the rest of us will never be able to understand what the argument was all about, any more than we can understand why a particular Prokofiev composition is a "formalistic perversion" or why spanking your daughter-in-law is a rightist deviation. We do know that this ideological intrusion into physics actually slowed down Soviet progress in this field for a time.

But gradually, and most conspicuously after the death of Stalin, *in the one carefully circumscribed area of physical science, the dread virus of freedom of thought was turned loose.*

We have seen the results.

And we have witnessed the upside-down conclusion drawn by Soviet spokesmen. They would like us to believe that the launching of earth satellites is somehow a triumph of Communism. It would be nearer the truth to say that it is a demonstration of what the enterprise principle of freedom of thought can do when released among a talented and determined people.

In addition to these three examples—productivity, incentive, and freedom of thought—other illustrations could be given to elaborate the same point. Thus, the very un-Communistic principle of decentralization has been spreading rapidly throughout the Communist world. In 1957 for example, everyday decisions affecting the Soviet industrial system were almost entirely decentralized and assigned to the Regional Economic Councils.

But the examples given will serve to illustrate the main points, which are that—whatever may be the case with attitudes and emotions—the basic facts of life even in the Communist countries are bringing them nearer to what we are for, and that, therefore, these facts are giving us at least the raw materials out of which greater identification and understanding can be fashioned.

In other words, a kind of identification *in fact* is taking place, but it has not been matched with intellectual and emotional identification.

But there may be those who, while readily accepting the desirabiilty of identification with free-world and "uncommitted" peoples, wonder whether identification should also be our ultimate goal in relation to the people of the Soviet bloc. This question must be faced, since the "cold war" has created in many minds in many countries an unspoken assumption that the goal, far from being identification, is rather the unconditional defeat of an enemy. In many other minds the preoccupation with each day's troubles is so engrossing that there is no time for formulating goals at all—no time to ask, "How does it all come out in the end?"

The Third Act

Sometimes nowadays when one listens to discussions of what to do about the world's tensions and conflicts, one cannot help being reminded of the kind of playwright who has a terrific idea for Act One and Act Two—but has simply not yet got round to thinking about how the story is going to be resolved in Act Three.

This thoughtless playwright readily establishes his plot's basic conflict in Act One. As Act Two progresses, each element in the conflict grows stronger, and the participants in the drama proceed to align themselves with the two main forces. There are stormy scenes. There are vigorous assertions of power and pride. The contesting characters dig themselves in deeper and deeper.

Now, if the author waits until he has written the play up to this point before asking himself, "How am I going to get them all out of this?" he will probably never be able to write the ending; or, if he does write it, it will not make much sense.

In our unfolding drama of the Destiny of Man, the people of the world have been writing in two plot lines.

In the one plot line, more and more misunderstanding seems to pile up, particularly between the Soviets and the United States.

In the other plot line, more and more weapons are piled up—weapons that will ensure that any possible Armageddon resulting from these misunderstandings will be absolute.

Where is the happy ending that follows logically from these diverging plot lines?

If these paths are followed out to their logical conclusion, is there even a hypothetical theory which could in the long run bring us, by these routes, to anything but catastrophe?

This is no children's tale in which the author can salvage an impossible plot and put everything right by having a fairy godmother change the dragon into Prince Charming with a touch of a magic wand. This is modern realistic drama.

If the final tragedy is not to take place, it is up to us—all of us in the world—to recognize the third plot line and make it the dominant one: the plot line of identification. We must figure out *now* the kind of outcome we want to see and start working our way toward it without delay.

In other words, we should have a clear picture of what

we are for on a global scale—a working pattern of the kind of world we want to see emerge. We should then help along any movement or trend, from whatever source and under whatever label, that brings the *substance* of that kind of world nearer.

Thus, if the substance of what we are for—freedom of thought, incentive, productivity—is indeed being adopted in the Soviet bloc, even though in a fragmentary and mislabeled version, we should welcome this development and commend its accomplishments as confirming our own principles and increasing the chances of ultimate understanding.

If the world we long for is a world in which opportunities for good education are widespread, and in which a self-reliant educated class provides a group with whom we can most readily achieve a meeting of minds, we should commend and help advance the rapid progress of education both in the newly developing countries and in the Communist bloc.

If the world we look for is a world of swiftly-advancing opportunities for industrial and agricultural advance by newly developing countries, and if we really believe that prosperity and progress favor the growth of what we are for and disfavor the growth of Communism—then, provided there are adequate safeguards against political subversion, we should welcome the offer of economic aid to these countries even when it comes from the Soviet Union.

If the world we seek is one which lives under a rule of law that governs even the disputes between nations, then we should bend every effort to make the most of any small beginnings in this direction.

If the world we yearn for is a world of harmony rather than hatred, we must create a people-to-people understanding between our own people and the people of countries now estranged from us.

It is up to us to see that the truth about what we stand for and are trying to do is accurately and effectively presented to people around the world, not least those in the Communist lands—many of whom apparently actually believe that the United States wants war and hopes to destroy the Russian nation and people.

This means that, having analyzed and articulated what we are for, we must be prepared to use every medium and vehicle of communication, identification, and understanding as fully as the particular people are ready to accept—radio, television, moving pictures, magazines, newspapers, news services, pamphlets, books, libraries, reading rooms, lectures, educational aids, English teaching, seminars, exhibits, shows, concerts, trade, tourism, exchanges of students and other persons, and such efforts as those of the People-to-People program.

We must not treat these activities as routine operations that can be merely continued at some fixed level adopted in the past. Are there plans to invite five Russian students to the United States? Why not five thousand?

Of course, all this is not in itself enough to guarantee long-range peace. The results must be reflected in the policies of governments.

This drawing together of peoples cannot and should not take the form of any sacrificing of our basic ideals nor of compromise with the expanionist tenets or repressive practices of the rulers of international Communism. One can only hope that, as this understanding between peoples becomes fuller and sounder, little by little the attitudes and actions of their governments will become adjusted to the real desires of the people until some day, perhaps, the governments themselves will be of a kind that we can live with in genuine harmony. But this process will take place only if we are firm, confident, and strong in upholding our basic ideas at home and around the world.

No one can say with certainty what will be the outcome of the evolutionary processes now going on within the

Soviet Union. The extent to which those processes effectively transform the official expansionist line of the Soviet government will determine, probably more than any other factor, the chances of peace in the world.

We have seen that the deepest wants and motivations of people are much the same everywhere. And now, all over the world, and notably in the Communist bloc, there are evidences that the people themselves are more and more asserting these basic aspirations, and, subject to many ups and downs, are on the whole succeeding more and more in getting them respected.

A new class of people is growing up—educated, accustomed to deal in real facts, and not inclined to be pushed around too much by anybody. The traditional wild-eyed Bolshevik, with beard and homemade bomb, is certainly not now an accurate symbol of the influential class in Russia. Increasingly, we are seeing the rise of the manager, the army man, the professional man, the scientist, the engineer, the educator, the successful artist, the inquisitive and confident student—all in all, a growing group who by the nature of their training and work must learn to work with real facts, at least in some fields, and accordingly cannot forever be expected to swallow the ideological fairy tales, historical inventions, charges of "capitalist" menace, and wildly improbable anti-American fictions on which they have been fed for so many years.

The Russian rulers have taken a gigantic gamble in unleashing the chain-reacting power of free thought—in the one area of sciences useful to the State. Can freedom of thought be confined to a single area? It is significant that one of the most pervasive themes of nineteenth-century Russian writing was the contention that man is an integral and indivisible creature, and that nothing he is or does is without its effect upon everything else he is or does. He cannot be one thing as a baker and another thing as a brother.

Against this backdrop of philosophy, the Soviet man cannot be expected to go on forever with a mind half slave and half free. For freedom is not a sometime thing.

Not only freedom of thought, but also independent economic power will apparently continue to grow in the U. S. S. R. Eventually we may see the crucial combination—substantial economic power joining political power, in the hands of large numbers of individuals with independent ideas—and the ingredients of evolutionary change toward a freer regime will be at hand.

We have observed earlier that a dictatorial absolutist regime cannot exist side by side with a modern economy geared to producing a widely shared abundance of good

171

things for people. A consumer-based economy can function only with the aid of an entire array of institutionalized freedoms—freedom to bargain, to trade, to invest, to hire and be hired, to organize, to compete, to innovate, to profit, to strike. The evolutionary change toward a prosperous consumer economy, if it ever comes about, will therefore be accompanied by an evolution toward a different kind of political economy. Eventually it will be all one thing or all another: either political dictation, expansionism, and subordination of consumer needs, or consumer prosperity, abandonment of expansionism, and greater internal political freedom.

The story can still go either way.

It is still not too late for us, as coauthors of this drama, to write into the plot as a dominant and controlling element the theme of genuine reciprocal understanding between people.

All this, of course, is only one segment of the total problem. For, even after understanding between people has been reached and translated into the policies of governments, these policies in turn must be applied to such concrete acts as creating an increasingly effective United Nations and World Court, negotiating authentic armament controls, handling skillfully the endless tensions and collisions that arise between national interests, and mak-

172

ing resort to the rule of law as normal and effective for international disputes as it is now for domestic ones.

To the cold appraisal of pure reason, this task may seem hopeless in its immensity and complexity.

But to anyone with religious faith, of whatever kind, it is unthinkable to suppose that the Creator has brought the human race through countless centuries of hard-won progress toward civilization and fulfillment, only to see the whole story end with a few sick and deformed creatures crawling about on a charred, reeking, radioactive cinder that once was a world.

Rather, men may some day conclude that the intense rivalry of this period, the competition to aid the less-developed countries, the effort to demonstrate superiority in production and standard of living and culture and ideas, the competitive programs of health, education, sanitation, agricultural modernization, and industrial improvement for hundreds of millions of long-neglected people, were all perhaps the Creator's way of hastening the advent of self-realization and the good life for all men.